KIDDING Around®

MIAMI

WHAT TO DO, WHERE TO GO, AND HOW TO HAVE FUN IN MIAMI

by Frank Davies

John Muir Publications

Santa Fe, New Mexico

John Muir Publications,
P.O. Box 613, Santa Fe, NM 87504

Printed in the United States of America
First edition. First printing October 1997

ISBN: 1-56261-372-3

Editors Peg Goldstein, Willow Older
Graphics Editor Steve Dietz
Production Janine Lehmann
Cover Design Caroline Van Remortel
Typesetting Kathleen Sparkes, White Hart Design
Illustrations Stacy Venturi-Pickett
Maps Susan Harrison
Activities Peg Goldstein
Printers Hi-Liter Graphics/Burton & Mayer
Cover Photo © Andre Jenny/Unicorn Stock Photos
Back Cover Photo © Robin Hill, Greater Miami CVB

Distributed to the book trade by
Publishers Group West
Emeryville, California

*While every effort has been made to provide accurate,
up-to-date information, the author and publisher accept
no responsibility for loss, injury, or inconvenience
sustained by any person using this book.*

About the Author

Frank Davies has been an editor and reporter with
The Miami Herald for more than 20 years. He lives
in Miami with his wife and son.

C O N T E N T S

COLOR THE ROUTE
FROM YOUR HOMETOWN TO MIAMI

If you're flying, color the states you'll fly over. If you're driving,
color the states you'll drive through. If you live in
Miami or Florida, color the states you have visited.

WELCOME TO MIAMI!

MIAMI, FLORIDA, IS ONE OF THE MOST exciting, special places in the United States. It's a great place to visit if you like being outdoors. Just imagine, you can go swimming and get a suntan on New Year's Day—when most of the rest of the country is shivering through winter.

⬆ **Miami's beaches are the best!**

That's because Miami has a unique climate. It's almost always warm. It can be very hot and humid in summer, when your clothes stick to your skin. But the rest of year is more comfortable. Miami's warm climate and beautiful beaches attract millions of visitors, as well as people who want to live here all the time.

The area is also special because it has plants and animals that you probably haven't seen before. If you're an explorer, a wilderness area called the Everglades is right next door.

INDIANS AND PIONEERS

The first people to live in Miami were the Tequesta Indians, who discovered the area more than 10,000 years ago. Spanish adventurers, settlers, and pirates explored the Miami area starting in the 1500s.

Seminole Indians and a related tribe, the Miccosukees, came to Florida in the 1800s. For a long time there was a war between the Indians and the United States Army. About 100 years ago, more settlers, including African Americans from the Bahamas, made Miami their home. The city began to grow.

The first major settlement was in Coconut Grove, just south of what is now downtown Miami. You can visit some old houses there and learn how people lived before air conditioning and bug spray.

⬆ These young people are Miccosukee Indians who lived in Miami in the early twentieth century.

The name Miami comes from the Indian word for "sweet water." The name referred to freshwater that comes down the Miami River from the Everglades.

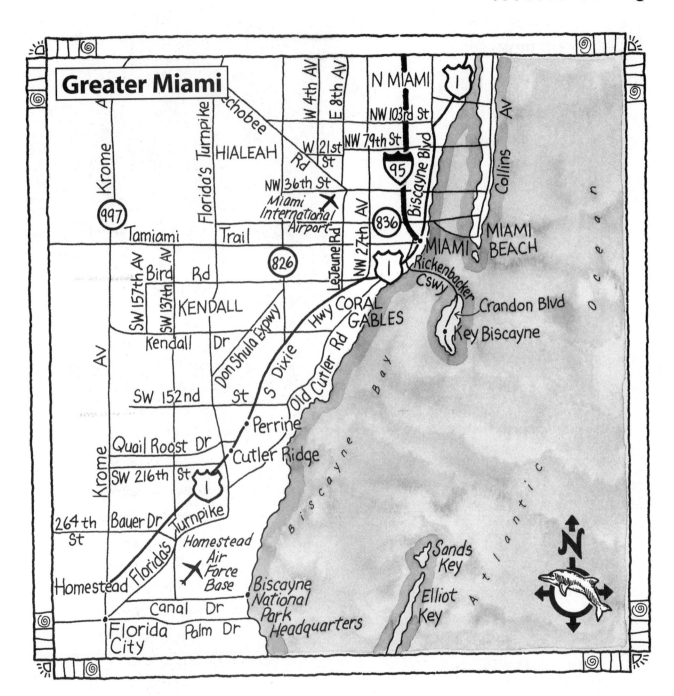

A City is Born

Miami is the youngest big city in the United States. It celebrated its 100th birthday in 1996. One of Miami's most famous residents is older than the city. Marjory Stoneman Douglas, who worked hard to preserve the Everglades, recently turned 106.

Miami started to grow when one of its pioneers, Julia Tuttle, persuaded a wealthy businessman, Henry Flagler, to extend his railroad all the way south to Miami. The area really got popular in the 1920s, when

⬆ **An old Miami farm from the days before cars and skyscrapers**

Many of the tiny islands you see in Biscayne Bay between Miami Beach and Miami were not there 100 years ago. The islands were made by people, and many homes were built there in the 1920s.

Northerners realized how warm Miami was in winter. They built big hotels and new homes in nearby Miami Beach and Coral Gables.

When you stand surrounded by skyscrapers downtown, it's hard to imagine what Miami looked like 100 years ago. There were just a few small buildings, an Indian trading post, and a dense rain forest back then.

THE CITY TODAY

Many American cities have immigrants—people who come from other countries. The Miami area, with more than 2 million people, may be home to the largest number of immigrants in the United States. More than half the people who live here were born in other countries—mainly Cuba, Haiti, Nicaragua, Colombia, and other Latin American nations.

⇧ **Storytelling at the Lowe Art Museum**

As you visit places in Miami, you will hear many people speaking Spanish. You will hear people from Haiti speaking Creole and people from Brazil speaking Portuguese. Many Cubans and Haitians left their countries in the last 30 years, seeking a better life in the United States.

So when you come to Miami, you're learning not just about an American city, but also about many foreign countries and cultures. You can try many foods from foreign countries, too.

A SPECIAL AREA

There's a lot about Miami that is unique. Outside of Hawaii, it's the only subtropical (almost tropical) place in the United States. It has wilderness areas such as the Everglades and animals such as panthers and manatees that are found in few other places.

The Everglades is a vast "river of grass." When viewed from the air, it looks like an endless swamp. It's home to dangerous reptiles, such as alligators and snakes, and beautiful wading birds. The Everglades provides freshwater to south Florida.

Over the years, people have been careless about protecting the Everglades. Hunters almost killed off some of the animals there, including alligators and panthers.

Now a big project is underway to protect the Everglades and its animals.

⇑ **Boardwalks allow people to experience the Everglades up close.**

The alligator is making a comeback. In fact, there are now so many alligators in the Everglades that hunting is allowed again. But the Florida panther and the manatee, a slow-moving sea creature, are still in great danger.

Rare sea turtles, manatees, and panthers can now be tracked by radio. Scientists put electronic collars or bands on the animals, then follow where they go. By learning more about where the animals live and travel, scientists can do more to protect them.

Miami Area

Gratigny Pkwy

OPA-LOCKA

Opa-Locka Blvd

NW 135th St

NW 119th St

NORTH MIAMI

W Dixie Hwy

Sunny Isles Blvd

NW 103rd St

HIALEAH

E 8th AV

Biscayne Blvd

Broad Cswy

Biscayne

John F Kennedy

NW 79th St

Cswy

Bay

27th AV

NW 62nd St

Miami AV

N

U.S. 27

Okeechobee Rd

Airport Expressway

Julia Tuttle

Collins AV

MIAMI BEACH

836

MIAMI

Cswy

Venetian

Dolphin Expwy

LeJeune Rd

Cswy

Mac Arthur Cswy

W Flagler St

41 Trail

SW 37th NW

1

Dixie Hwy

S Bayshore Dr

Rickenbacker

Tamiami

Ocean

Atlantic

Cswy

Bird Rd

CORAL GABLES

South

COCONUT GROVE

Crandon Blvd

KEY BISCAYNE

GATEWAY TO THE AMERICAS

Miami has earned the title "Gateway to the Americas," and if you look at a map of the Western Hemisphere, you can see why. Miami is the closest U.S. city to most of Latin America.

Miami's airport is one of the busiest in the United States, with direct flights from Latin America, Europe, and even South Africa. In fact, more foreign visitors—more than 3 million a year—come to Miami than to any other American city. There are also millions of visitors who come from other American cities.

Latin Americans love visiting Miami, even in the hot summer. That's because when it's summer in Miami, it's winter in countries such as Brazil and Argentina.

When you're in the downtown area, you will probably see large cruise ships and freighters. Miami's port is one of the biggest in the country.

GETTING AROUND

Once you're in Miami, your family will probably need a car to get around. You can use trains called the Metrorail and Metromover to get to the downtown attractions, but places such as Metrozoo and the Everglades are 20 miles away or more.

There are other ways to get around in Miami, especially in Biscayne Bay. You can take "water taxis" from Miami Beach to Bayside and other places. These small boats will take you past giant cruise ships and strange-looking seaplanes that land right on the water.

There's also a railroad network called Tri-Rail that links Miami to the two counties to the north, Broward and Palm Beach.

WEATHER AND HURRICANES

The weather in Miami has had a big impact on its history and growth. Henry Flagler built a railroad to Miami in 1896 when he learned that it was warm enough to grow citrus fruits all year. The warm winter weather has also attracted thousands of people to move here, often after they retire.

The most dangerous weather events in Miami are hurricanes. Everybody keeps a close eye on the Atlantic Ocean and the Caribbean Sea from August to November, when these powerful storms form.

⬆ **Hurricane Andrew destroyed boats, cars, and houses.**

If you come to Miami between June and October, prepare for two things— strong sun and lots of rain. Always wear sunscreen! The rainiest month in Miami's history was October 1908, when 28 inches fell!

Sometimes the winds in a hurricane are faster than 150 miles per hour. One hurricane in 1926 killed hundreds of people and destroyed much of the young city. In 1992 Hurricane Andrew caused $30 billion in damage in south Florida. Many communities are still recovering from the storm.

Since people can track and prepare for hurricanes, they are sometimes less dangerous than earthquakes and tornadoes. The National Hurricane Center, located in Miami, uses satellites, airplanes, and computers to follow the storms and predict where they will go.

FAMOUS FACES

Because of the warm weather, people have always been attracted to Miami. Some of the people are famous and some are infamous! In the 1930s gangsters such as Al Capone spent their winters here.

Presidents have been coming here for years. One man who ran for president three times (and always lost) settled in Coral Gables in the 1920s. He was William Jennings Bryan. President Harry Truman had a home in Key West, and John Kennedy had a home near Palm

⇧ **Sylvester Stallone calls the Miami area home.**

Beach. When Richard Nixon was president, his "winter White House" was on Key Biscayne.

Movie and music stars have been coming here since early in the 20th century. Johnny Weissmuller, the original movie Tarzan, performed water shows in the Venetian Pool. Today, Madonna, Sylvester Stallone, Gloria Estefan, and Michael Caine live here. Miami is also a favorite place to make movies.

Gloria Estefan, here with her husband Emilio, is a popular Cuban American singer.

WEATHER OR NOT

Wanda is giving a weather report, and she is confused about which storm is headed toward Miami. Which kind of storm are you most likely to see in Miami?

PARKS AND THE GREAT OUTDOORS

IN MIAMI YOU CAN SWIM AT SOME OF THE BEST beaches in the world. You can float in a huge pool, through a grotto (or cave) carved out of limestone rock. Then, when you really want to explore, there's a vast wilderness area called the Everglades not far away. It has animals that you might think belong in the Amazon rain forest.

⬆ **Lighthouse at Biscayne National Park**

There are many different ways to see the Everglades: by foot, on trams, on bikes, and even in canoes. There's also an unusual method of transportation called the airboat. Some say it was invented in south Florida. It looks like a big raft with a large propeller on the back.

Wherever you go outdoors, remember to bring two things: sunscreen and bug spray. Even in winter, when it's not as hot, the powerful sun can burn you. And in summer, you have to watch out for mosquitoes in wilderness areas.

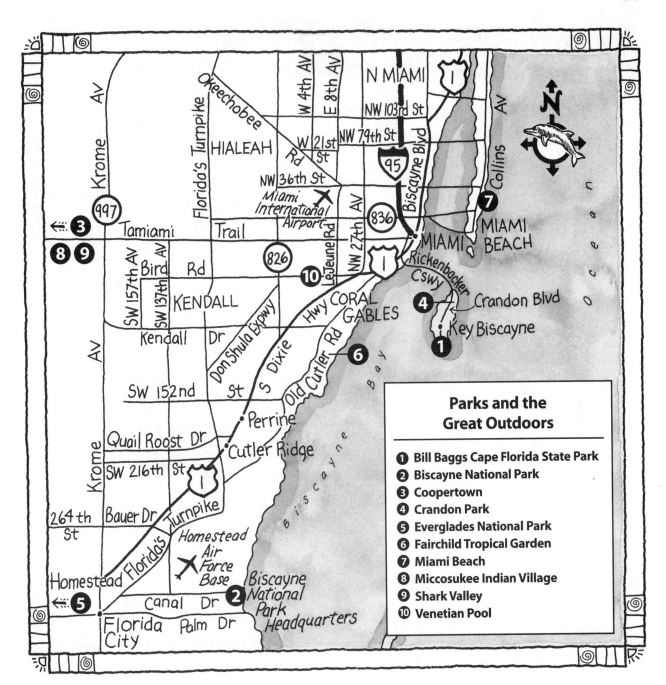

Parks and the Great Outdoors

1. Bill Baggs Cape Florida State Park
2. Biscayne National Park
3. Coopertown
4. Crandon Park
5. Everglades National Park
6. Fairchild Tropical Garden
7. Miami Beach
8. Miccosukee Indian Village
9. Shark Valley
10. Venetian Pool

BEACH AT KEY BISCAYNE

There are more than 15 miles of beautiful beaches near Miami, and two of the best are on Key Biscayne, an island close to downtown. When you drive to Key Biscayne on the Rickenbacker Causeway, look behind you for one of the best views of the city.

To get to the beaches, you'll go past a revolving shark sculpture and the **Seaquarium**. The first beach is **Crandon Park**, which has a good snack bar, plenty of parking, and an old-fashioned carousel.

At the southern tip of Key Biscayne is **Bill Baggs Cape Florida State Park**. Large shade trees and lots of tables give you room to spread out for picnics. Many tall pine trees here were knocked down by Hurricane Andrew, but new trees have been planted.

At the tip of Cape Florida State Park is a lighthouse, built in the early 1800s. It was once attacked by Indians.

⇡ **The beach can get crowded at Key Biscayne.**

⇡ **Picnic under a palm tree at Crandon Park Beach.**

WHICH FISH?

These five kids are fishing. But their fishing lines got tangled. How are they going to find out what they caught? Trace each line to the bottom and you'll find out.

MIAMI BEACH

The beach at Miami Beach is nice, but be ready for a long walk to the ocean. Many years ago storms washed away a lot of the sand here. So crews dredged sand from the ocean floor and added it to the beach. The extra sand makes the beach very wide.

↥ **Hotels, stores, and restaurants line the shore at Miami Beach.**

Miami Beach has many restaurants, snack bars, and stores. There are places to rent umbrellas, in-line skates, and bikes. There's a pathway for bikes and skaters right along the ocean.

North of Miami Beach is **Haulover Beach**, which usually isn't crowded. At Haulover, you can fish from a long pier or fly a kite.

If you see something that looks like a blue plastic bag washed up on the beach, don't touch it. It's probably a man-of-war, a type of jellyfish that stings.

TEST YOUR SPANISH

Miami is a great place to learn Spanish. Draw a line to match the English word with the correct Spanish one. Here are some clues to help you.

ENGLISH

SPANISH

sun

árbol

book

sol

water

agua

tree

libro

Clue Box

aquarium
Arbor Day
library
solar system

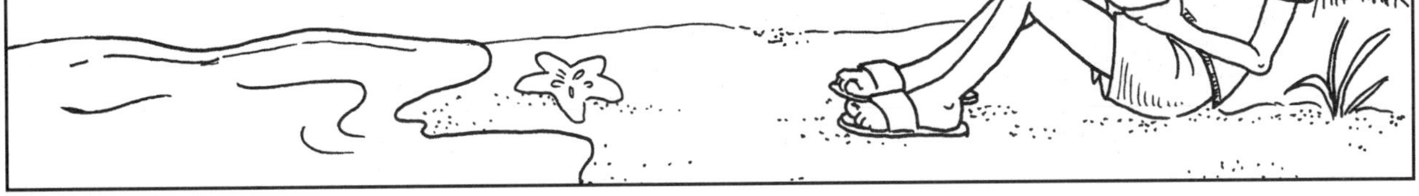

EVERGLADES NATIONAL PARK

From the air, the Everglades looks like a vast swamp. Actually, it's a slow-moving river—just a few inches deep and 50 miles wide. Alligators, colorful birds, snakes, and fish live here.

People are fighting to preserve the Everglades and its animals.

Everglades National Park, about 45 miles south of Miami, covers 1.5 million acres. It's the biggest wilderness area east of the Rocky Mountains.

There's a new visitor center at the Homestead entrance to the park, with movies and exhibits. Park rangers and scientists lead tours, hikes, and canoe trips. On the road to the town of Flamingo, there are boardwalks and observation towers. In Flamingo you can rent bikes and boats, take a trip on a schooner, and stay overnight.

Visit the Shark Valley entrance to the park, about 30 miles west of Miami. You can walk or ride a bike very close to the birds and alligators. Despite its name, there are no sharks in Shark Valley!

The Everglades is the most important breeding ground for tropical wading birds in North America. Look for the purple gallinule—it's very colorful.

EVERGLADES WORD SEARCH

Hidden in this word search are some words that describe the Everglades or things you might see there. Search for words vertically, horizontally, and diagonally. Can you find all 11 words? One word has been found for you.

Word Box

alligator	wilderness	panther
snake	bird	tropical
airboat	park	river
manatee	canoe	

```
A I R B O A T E S O P M Y P Z
H P A N T H E R Y M S N A K E
N Y N L S G A I O N P T L B O
T T P O D P S V A P I N L U L
R A T C M M A E D V I E I T E
D E U E A D F R G N N C G T Y
E D S R N N A N K U I U A E D
S A X S A C O Q D K C L T L A
P O N D T K R E W B O A O F L
U I S E E S U R N P B I R D Z
W I L D E R N E S S L I M Y N
D Y D N I O P Y C R T M B E L
```

BISCAYNE NATIONAL PARK

Biscayne National Park is unusual because most of it is underwater, or right on the water. Here's your chance to explore a deep green forest of mangroves from a canoe or bigger boat. Mangroves grow along the shoreline, and their strong roots provide homes for birds, turtles, and other animals.

You can stop by the visitor center, take a ride in glass-bottom boat, or go snorkeling and diving. You can rent kayaks and canoes, go fishing, or camp overnight on one of the islands in Biscayne Bay.

There is a lot of farmland between Biscayne and Everglades National Parks. In winter, you might be able to pick your own strawberries and other fruit. Visit one of many produce stands, such as **Robert Is Here**, and sample a delicious milk shake made with key limes.

⬆ **Snorkelers see Miami from a different angle.**

All sorts of rare fruit grows in south Florida. One kind is *Monstera deliciosa*, which looks like a large, green ear of corn but tastes like banana and pineapple.

⬅ **Explore the shore.**

WHAT DO YOU SEE?

If you were one of the kids on this boat, what do you think you'd see in the ocean near Florida? Draw the things you might see, including animals, plants—maybe even sunken treasure!

FAIRCHILD TROPICAL GARDEN

⬆ **Kids use magnifiers to examine tiny tropical plants.**

Here's your chance to explore a tropical paradise. Fairchild Tropical Garden is filled with rare plants and jungle plants. Fairchild is close to downtown Miami. So if you don't get a chance to go the Everglades, Fairchild can give you a taste of what the Everglades is like.

A tram takes you through sunken gardens, a rain forest display, and one of the world's largest collections of palm trees. On weekends there are concerts and plant sales. You can buy a tropical plant. Imagine a purple orchid on your windowsill.

Next door to Fairchild is a small park called **Matheson Hammock**. It has climbing trees, a picnic area, and a lagoon for swimming. There are no waves, so this is a good place to swim if you are just learning.

Fairchild Garden has the largest collection of tropical plants and trees in the continental United States.

HIDE & SEEK

How many animals can you find in this tropical scene? Many animals blend in well with the ground and plants. So be sure to look hard!

INDIANS AND AIRBOATS

What's it like to skim across the Everglades with the wind in your face and a roaring engine behind you? You can find out at the **Miccosukee Indian Village** about 30 miles west of Miami.

↥ **Airboats take you on a wild ride.**

The Miccosukee Indians have lived in the Everglades for many years. They make crafts, "wrestle" alligators, and take visitors on tours. The village has a small museum, a restaurant, and a gift shop.

On **Tamiami Trail** there are about ten different places to ride airboats, originally called "swamp gliders." Put some cotton in your ears when the tour guides pass it around, because airboats are very noisy when they reach speeds of 40 miles per hour or more.

Coopertown has a small restaurant where you can try two kinds of food caught right outside—frogs' legs and "gator" meat.

The Tamiami Trail got its name from the cities of Tampa and Miami. When the trail was built many years ago, it was the only road connecting the two cities.

LATER, GATOR

How many words can you make using the
letters in the word ALLIGATOR? An example
to help get you started is the word TAIL.
Write your answers below.

A L L I G A T O R

Tail

VENETIAN POOL

Dive into Venetian Pool in Coral Gables and you might end up in a cave, listening to the echo of your own voice and watching shadows on smooth limestone walls. Or you might splash and climb your way through a small waterfall and pretend you're a tropical explorer.

The Venetian Pool was carved out of limestone bedrock in 1923. This huge pool makes for some of the best swimming around. Because the water comes from underground springs, it's always cool—even on the hottest days in summer.

The area around Venetian Pool looks like Venice, a city in Italy. There are colorful barber poles, tiled roofs, and even a cobblestone bridge to a wading area. There's a nice beach and a snack bar.

Exotic Venetian Pool

Venetian Pool is one of the biggest pools you will ever swim in. It holds 800,000 gallons of water.

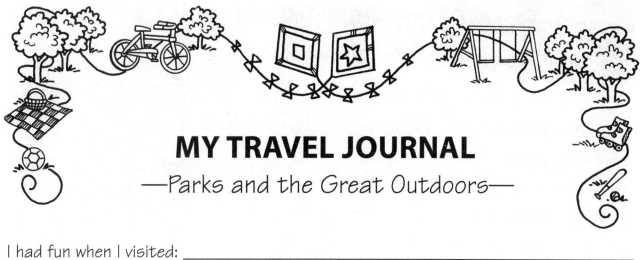

MY TRAVEL JOURNAL
—Parks and the Great Outdoors—

I had fun when I visited: _____

I learned about: _____

My favorite park was: _____

This is a picture of what I saw at a park in Miami

3 ANIMALS, ANIMALS

BECAUSE OF SOUTH FLORIDA'S SUBTROPICAL CLIMATE, it has interesting wildlife—from dolphins to alligators to panthers. Some of these animals are endangered, but others are doing well. There are a few places here where you can see animals up close and touch them.

Since Miami is such a warm place, animals from other hot regions—parrots from South America, tigers from India—can thrive here. That's why Miami built a zoo with a great collection of animals from South America, Asia, and Africa.

⬆ **Chimps at Monkey Jungle**

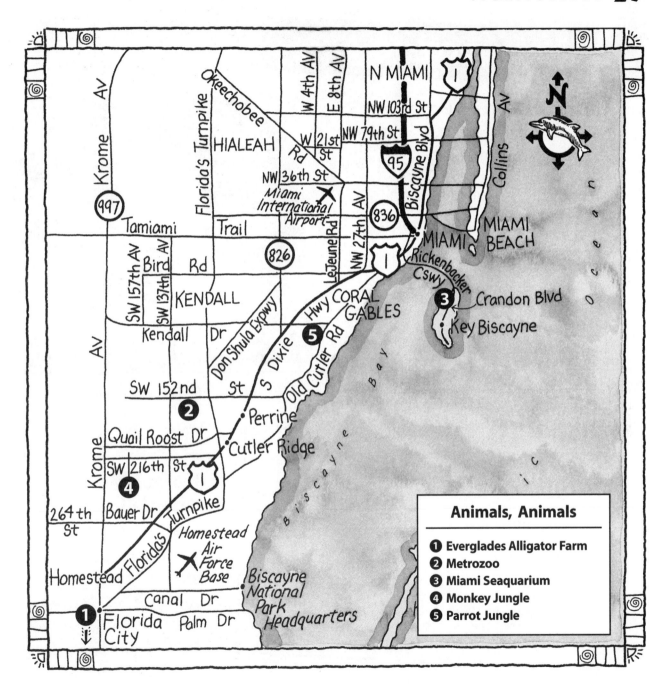

Animals, Animals

① Everglades Alligator Farm
② Metrozoo
③ Miami Seaquarium
④ Monkey Jungle
⑤ Parrot Jungle

METROZOO

Metrozoo is best known for being "cageless." That means the gorillas, rhinos, hippos, white Bengal tigers, and other animals roam large areas. You can walk to see all the animals. When your feet get tired, you can take a monorail around the entire zoo.

In a special area, you can get close to some of the animals, such as koala bears from Australia and a slithery albino python from South America. A special exhibit shows you one of the biggest lizards in the world—the Komodo dragon from Indonesia (it's not really a dragon). Wait until you see its tongue!

Watch for the elephant show. You may get to ride an elephant, one of the largest land creatures in the world. You can also touch small animals in a petting zoo.

Metrozoo has some fascinating animals, such as this white tiger.

Hurricane Andrew destroyed parts of Metrozoo, killed five mammals, and knocked over many trees. Almost all the animals, including 200 birds, were saved.

ENORMOUS ELEPHANTS

Draw yourself sitting on this elephant and imagine what it would feel like to ride such a big animal. Afterward, color the scene.

MIAMI SEAQUARIUM

↥ Leaping Lolita!

The Seaquarium includes manatees. Because of boat collisions and disease, there are only a few hundred manatees left in Florida.

If you're interested in marine creatures, this is the place for you. The Seaquarium, which is close to the beaches on Key Biscayne, has super ocean wildlife shows.

When you watch Lolita, a huge black-and-white killer whale, leap out of the water, get ready for a splash many times bigger than any cannonball you could make. People sitting close to the Lolita shows often get soaked.

The sea lions show that they're natural comedians. If you're lucky, you might get to feed them.

Watch the dolphins and see how they communicate with their trainers. Many of the dolphins you see have been TV and movie stars.

Get a schedule of feeding times. Through glass, you can watch hammerhead sharks and large sea turtles munching on lunch.

MATCHING FUN

In the picture, there are two different kinds of sharks, two different kinds of whales, and two different kinds of dolphins. Draw a line between the animals that go together.

EVERGLADES ALLIGATOR FARM

From 5-inch babies to 6-foot giants, this is the place to see the best-known animal in Florida—the alligator. Everglades Alligator Farm, near the entrance to the national park, is a real farm that raises alligators. It has more than 2,000 gators. Some are in special pens, and you can get very close to them.

⇑ **See an alligator eye to eye.**

Every day the farm has gator shows, where wildlife experts "wrestle" with the animals and tell you all about them. You can even hold a baby gator. The farm also has snakes, bears, crocodiles, bobcats, and raccoons.

You can take an airboat ride at the farm and spot gators, turtles, ospreys, snowy egrets, and other animals. The driver might even do a couple of spins and sharp turns. If you sit in front, be ready to get wet.

⇚ **Are you brave enough to hold a gator?**

Many years ago, hunters almost killed off all the alligators. Now there are more than one million—just in Florida.

UNSCRAMBLE THE ANIMALS

LGOALTRIA _____

REBA _____

OCONRCA _____

NEKSA _____

RTELTU _____

Unscramble each word to find the name of an animal. When you are done, draw a line connecting each animal to the correct picture.

PARROT JUNGLE

Minutes after you enter Parrot Jungle, a bright blue macaw could be eating out of your hand. For a quarter, buy some sunflower seeds, stick out your hand, and hold still. You'll be surprised that these birds with their powerful beaks can nibble the food without nipping you.

The parrots squawk and talk and put on a great show. In a small theater, they ride bicycles, roller skate, and even do counting tricks. There's also a snake show, a playground, and a petting zoo. Watch out for the baby goats and pigs—they can almost knock you over trying to get to the food.

You can watch pink flamingoes wade through a lake, then check out the wildlife shows. One show, called "Creatures in the Mist," includes insects, reptiles, and mammals from the Amazon rain forest.

↑
Because Miami is near the tropics, parrots and other tropical birds are right at home here.

One of Parrot Jungle's most popular birds is Pinky, a bicycle-riding cockatoo. He's more than 50 years old and still performing.

Pinky is a star! ⇛

CONNECT THE DOTS

Connect the dots to find a special animal that likes water.
Then color the scene.

Squirrel monkeys are only about two feet long.

Monkey Jungle opened in 1933 with six macaques from Asia. There are now about 95 macaques— all descended from the original six.

MONKEY JUNGLE

Explore the screened walkways in Monkey Jungle, and you'll know what it feels like to walk through a rain forest, with hundreds of monkeys screeching overhead. You can put a little bit of food in a cup and watch a squirrel monkey carefully pull it up and eat it.

Some of Monkey Jungle's rare and endangered animals, such as long-armed gibbons from Asia and golden lion tamarins from Brazil, are kept in cages for their protection. The smallest monkeys, pygmy marmosets, weigh only about 4 ounces.

Animal shows begin every 30 minutes. King, a 450-pound lowland gorilla, is the star of one show. He can match numbers to show you his intelligence. One of the chimps might steal the show with his acrobatic antics.

MY TRAVEL JOURNAL

—Animals, Animals—

I had fun when I visited: _____

I learned about: _____

_____

My favorite animal was: _____

This is a picture of an animal I saw

 # LANDMARKS AND THE ARTS

DO YOU LIKE DIFFERENT KINDS OF MUSIC and art, especially with a tropical flavor? Would you like to explore a city on an elevated car that twists around corners and skyscrapers like an amusement-park ride?

Miami is a place to try new things. You can hear steel drums on the streets of Coconut Grove and at Lincoln Road Mall. You can hear Brazilian samba, Jamaican reggae, and Cuban salsa in the Bayfront Park Auditorium. There's a concert almost every weekend.

A famous dance company practices in a storefront, so you can see their every move. Art museums let you explore the world of paintings and sculptures.

⬆ **Miami's music scene is a blast!**

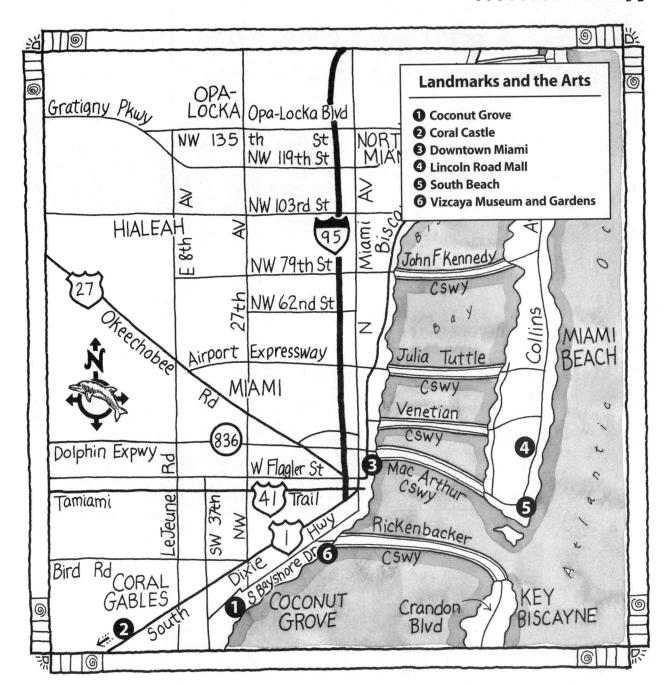

Landmarks and the Arts

1 **Coconut Grove**
2 **Coral Castle**
3 **Downtown Miami**
4 **Lincoln Road Mall**
5 **South Beach**
6 **Vizcaya Museum and Gardens**

Gratigny Pkwy

OPA-LOCKA

Opa-Locka Blvd

NW 135th St
NW 119th St

NORTH MIAMI

NW 103rd St

HIALEAH

E 8th AV

AV

95

NW 79th St

27th

NW 62nd St

27

Miami AV
N Biscayne AV

John F Kennedy Cswy

Bay

Julia Tuttle Cswy

Collins AV

MIAMI BEACH

Okeechobee Rd

Airport Expressway

MIAMI

836

Venetian Cswy

4

N

Dolphin Expwy

W Flagler St

41 Trail

3

Mac Arthur Cswy

Atlantic Ocean

5

Tamiami

LeJeune Rd

SW 37th NW

1 Dixie Hwy

S Bayshore Dr

Rickenbacker Cswy

Bird Rd

CORAL GABLES

6

1

COCONUT GROVE

Crandon Blvd

KEY BISCAYNE

2

South

Atlantic

COCONUT GROVE

Coconut Grove is one of Miami's oldest neighborhoods and one of its most interesting. Its restaurants, movie theaters, and stores are very popular. But even when the neighborhood's a little crowded, it's a great place for just walking around. You can also rent bikes and head down Main Highway, exploring hidden neighborhoods. Or you can grab an ice cream cone and watch for celebrities. Sylvester Stallone might be heading over to his Planet Hollywood restaurant.

⇑ **Nighttime in Coconut Grove**

There's a lot to see nearby, including the **Vizcaya Museum** and the **Miami Science Museum**. Almost every weekend Coconut Grove has an art or food festival, a parade, sometimes even a bed race on wheels!

If you like theater, visit the **Coconut Grove Playhouse** and the **Actors' Playhouse** in nearby Coral Gables. Both often put on special shows for kids.

The first African American settlement in Miami was in Coconut Grove. The settlers were immigrants from the Bahamas.

CROSSWORD FUN

Solve this crossword puzzle by figuring out the clues or completing the sentences. If you need help, use the clue box

Across
3. This kind of storm can be very dangerous.
5. _____ is a state in the southern United States.
8. This is a big, exciting city in Florida.

Down
1. The _____ is hot on Miami.
2. This sport is popular in Florida.
4. _____ trees are common in Florida.
6. This place has a lot of sand.
7. Summer in Miami can be _____.

Clue Box
sun   Florida
Miami   fishing
rainy   hurricane
beach   palm

SOUTH BEACH

If you walk down Ocean Drive on South Beach, you may see a little bit of everything, from an in-line skater with a parrot on each shoulder to the latest tattoos, hairstyles, and exotic clothes. Don't be surprised if you see photographers taking pictures of fashion models.

South Beach has become a popular gathering place. One good way to see it is by renting a bike or in-line skates. If you get hot, just walk across the beach for a dip in the Atlantic Ocean.

You will notice small hotels—built in the 1920s and 1930s—with an unusual, streamlined look. This style is called Art Deco. The buildings are part of a new historic district.

⇑ If you like unique buildings, you'll love South Beach.

Miami Beach used to be mostly for older people, but not anymore. The average age of a person living here was 65 in 1980. Ten years later the average age was 44.

⇚ Skaters love it here.

WHAT'S THE DIFFERENCE?

These two beaches might look the same, but they are not. How many differences between the two scenes can you find? Hint: There are at least 12 differences.

LINCOLN ROAD MALL

At Lincoln Road Mall, you can try your hand at painting, watch students and professionals practice ballet, listen to all kinds of music, and try foods from different countries.

The mall is an open area where people walk and skate, musicians play, and many restaurants have outdoor tables. You can watch through big glass windows as the **Miami City Ballet** tries some new moves. When the **New World Symphony** holds its concerts, the sound is projected outside.

In the middle of the mall is the **South Florida Art Center**, where more than 80 artists work and display their creations. On Saturday mornings the center holds classes and tours for kids.

⇧ **During the Halloween concert, kids learn about music from the pros.**

Lincoln Road is a great place the week before Halloween. Kids dress up in their favorite costumes for a concert of scary music by the New World Symphony.

SHOW TIME

**It's show time, but the symphony members need their instruments.
Draw a line from each musician to the proper instrument.**

DOWNTOWN

Miami is sometimes called the Magic City, and at sunset it's easy to see why. More than 40 skyscrapers downtown are lit up by powerful lights. There are lots of red, white, and blue lights on the Fourth of July and red and green lights at Christmas.

A great way to see downtown is to hop on the **Metromover**, an elevated train. The Metromover gives you a great view of **Freedom Tower** (which looks like it was built in Spain), big cruise ships, freighters on the Miami River, and the busy **Bayside Marketplace**. The Metromover can take you to the **Historical Museum of South Florida** and the **Miami Art Museum**. Best of all, the ride costs only a quarter.

↑ **Take a ride on the Metromover.**

Freedom Tower was Miami's first skyscraper, built in 1924. It became a symbol of freedom for many Cubans who fled to Florida from their country in the 1960s.

COLORING SURPRISE

There are many skyscrapers in Miami. Using one color, darken all the windows on this skyscraper that have the letters N, B, C, E, G, J, K, L, or P. When you're done, read the hidden message.

VIZCAYA MUSEUM AND GARDENS

Vizcaya is a spectacular mansion made to look like an old Italian palace. Early in the 1900s, a millionaire named James Deering traveled throughout Europe, getting ideas and furnishings for this huge house. He collected doors, ceilings, and fireplaces.

⬆ **Vizcaya is an awesome sight.**

His crew of 800 workers took five years to build Vizcaya. They finished it in 1916. While grownups might be most interested in the mansion and its antiques, you may like playing in the gardens best. The gardens are filled with statues and fountains.

Vizcaya hosts a colorful Renaissance fair every spring. President Ronald Reagan met Pope John Paul II at the mansion in 1987.

Vizcaya got its name from the Basque province of Spain. The name means "high place." Vizcaya overlooks Biscayne Bay, which is named for the Bay of Biscay in northern Spain.

A-MAZING GARDENS!

FINISH

START

These gardens are beautiful. But don't get lost here.
Can you help the visitors get through the maze to the mansion?

CORAL CASTLE

Coral Castle is a very unusual building south of Miami in Homestead. A man from Latvia named Edward Leedskalnin made this entire house out of coral rock—thousands of tons of it. He even made some furniture and a telescope out of coral. It took him 20 years to finish the house, which he did in 1921.

The mystery about Coral Castle is how one man, with very little help and no modern machines, could build such a place. Did Leedskalnin know some secrets of ancient technology? He used a complicated system of ropes and pulleys to get the job done.

⇡ Sculptures at Coral Castle

Engineers are still trying to figure out how parts of Coral Castle were made. They wonder about the 9-ton gate, for example, that you can open with a nudge.

MY TRAVEL JOURNAL
—Landmarks and the Arts—

I had fun when I visited: _____

I learned about: _____

My favorite building was: _____

This is a picture of a building I saw

5 GOOD SPORTS

From water sports to golf and tennis, Miami is a great place for the great outdoors. It's also a great place to see some of the best sports teams in the United States. Most of the time, you don't have to wear extra layers of clothing while you're watching a football or baseball game.

The oldest professional club in Miami is the Dolphins football team. They won two Super Bowls in the 1970s. Quarterback Dan Marino has set many records. The Florida Marlins baseball team added many new players in 1997 and became a better team. The Florida Panthers made people excited about hockey—especially when they made it to the Stanley Cup finals in only their third year. The Miami Heat basketball team features center Alonzo Mourning and a winning record.

⬆ **Marlins baseball is hot!**

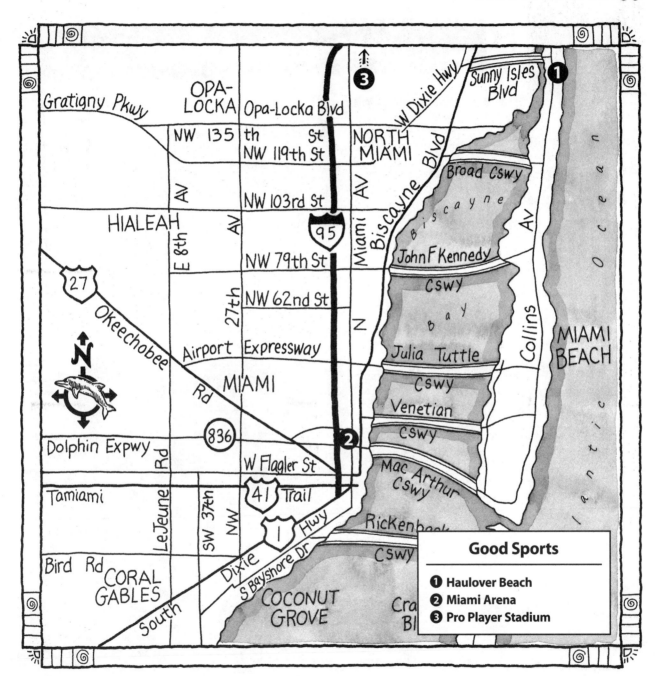

Good Sports

❶ Haulover Beach
❷ Miami Arena
❸ Pro Player Stadium

The new Dolphins coach, Jimmy Johnson, won a national college championship at the University of Miami and a Super Bowl at Dallas before returning to Miami.

MIAMI DOLPHINS

The Miami Dolphins have been playing exciting football since the team was formed in 1966. They're best known for having the only perfect season in pro football history: In 1972 they won all 17 games, including the Super Bowl. Former coach Don Shula won 347 games in his career, more than any other coach.

The Dolphins used to play their games in the Orange Bowl, a famous old stadium near downtown Miami. Now they play in Pro Player Stadium, about 20 miles north of Miami. During the preseason (July and August), you can visit the Dolphins' training camp and watch the players work out. Camp is in the town of Davie, about 25 miles northwest of Miami.

Dan Marino has made ⇛ the Dolphins great.

CREATE A CHEER

**Cheerleaders can really help a team win. Make up a cheer for the
Miami Dolphins or for your favorite team.**

FLORIDA MARLINS

The Florida Marlins baseball team has been a big hit since it joined the National League in 1993. It's easier to get a ticket for a Marlins game than for other professional games in Miami. You can often walk right up and buy a ticket.

The Marlins play their home games on natural grass in Pro Player Stadium. At many games the Marlins give away backpacks, caps, pins, and other souvenirs. Each year, starting in March, you can call or write the Marlins for a schedule, including giveaways. Ask about special ticket prices for kids.

If you go to a game in the middle of summer, remember, it will be very hot (that's why most games are played at night), and it can rain at any time. But most rain delays don't last long.

After some Marlins games, kids can run around the bases just like the players and even slide into home plate.

⬆ **A Marlin base runner gets ready to make his move.**

WHAT'S WRONG HERE?

Strange things are happening at the baseball game today.
Circle 13 things that are wrong with this picture.
When you're done, color the scene

FLORIDA PANTHERS

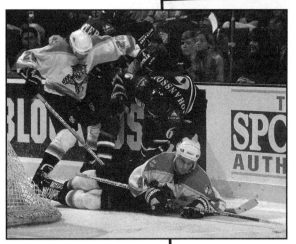

⇧ **There's no shortage of action at Panthers games.**

Who would think that a game played on ice would become so popular so fast in Florida! That's what happened when the Florida Panthers joined the National Hockey League in 1993. In 1996 they amazed hockey fans everywhere by beating older teams such as Pittsburgh and Philadelphia in the playoffs. They made it to the Stanley Cup finals, then lost to the Colorado Avalanche.

The Panthers play between October and April in the Miami Arena, which they share with the Miami Heat basketball team. By the year 2000, the Panthers will be playing in a new arena in Sunrise, a town just west of Fort Lauderdale. Hockey tickets can be hard to get, so call ahead. The Panthers usually sell a few tickets the day of a game.

The Panthers uniform is decorated with an X, formed by a hockey stick and a palm tree.

MATCHING FUN

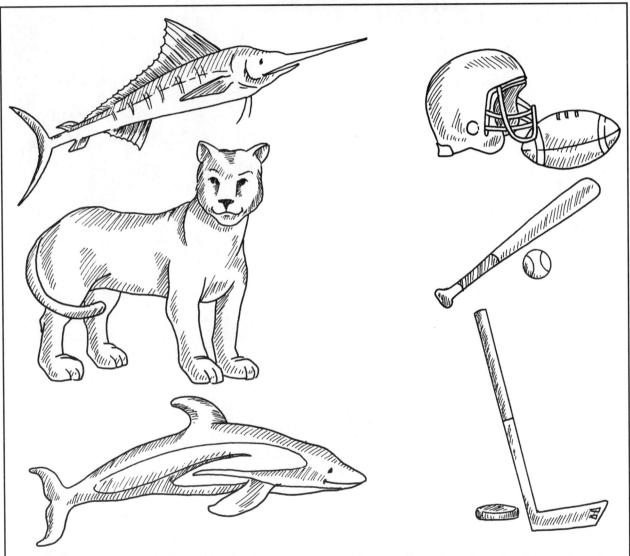

Florida has many sport teams named after animals. Match the animal with it's team's equipment.

MIAMI HEAT

The Miami Heat basketball team was created in 1988. If you watch a Heat game, you will notice that the team plays very good defense. They make it hard for the other team to score.

The Heat plays in the Miami Arena downtown. This arena is small. It has only 15,000 seats. So even the highest seats aren't too far from the court. You can usually get tickets a few days before a game. The team plans to move to a new, bigger arena in downtown Miami, next to the Bayside Marketplace shopping area.

One of the best things about a Heat game is watching Burnie, the Heat Mascot. He's a big, funny-looking fur ball with a basketball for a nose. He helps kids in races and contests, throws souvenir T-shirts into the stands, and sometimes steals the ball from the referee.

Alonzo Mourning soars to the net.

WORD SEARCH

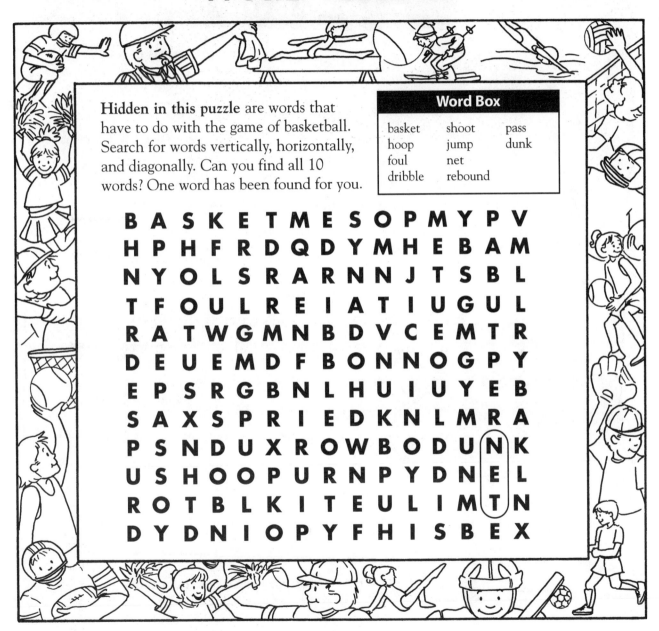

Hidden in this puzzle are words that have to do with the game of basketball. Search for words vertically, horizontally, and diagonally. Can you find all 10 words? One word has been found for you.

Word Box

basket	shoot	pass
hoop	jump	dunk
foul	net	
dribble	rebound	

```
B A S K E T M E S O P M Y P V
H P H F R D Q D Y M H E B A M
N Y O L S R A R N N J T S B L
T F O U L R E I A T I U G U L
R A T W G M N B D V C E M T R
D E U E M D F B O N N O G P Y
E P S R G B N L H U I U Y E B
S A X S P R I E D K N L M R A
P S N D U X R O W B O D U N K
U S H O O P U R N P Y D N E L
R O T B L K I T E U L I M T N
D Y D N I O P Y F H I S B E X
```

MORE MASCOTS

⬆ **Billy the Marlin shows his stuff.**

There is a tradition at Marlins baseball games. In the seventh inning, Billy the Marlin climbs on top of the dugout and leads everyone in singing "Take Me Out to the Ball Game." Billy looks sort of like a marlin, a fish that lives in the ocean. He does a lot of stunts during games. Sometimes he evens squirts water at the umpire or members of the other team.

The hockey team's name (Florida Panthers) and mascot (Stanley C. Panther) come from a famous Florida animal—the Everglades panther. There aren't too many panthers left in the wild, but there's always one prowling around the Miami Arena during hockey games. Imagine a panther that can slide on ice and use a slingshot to send souvenirs into the stands!

⬅ **What is Stanley C. Panther's middle name? Cup, of course, as in Stanley Cup!**

SCRAMBLED SONG

**Unscramble the letters to find the name
of a popular song at baseball games:**

KAET   _____

EM   _____

UTO   _____

OT   _____

ETH   _____

LMBAGALE   _____

FISHING

⇡ **You can fish from a boat or right from the shore.**

Haulover got its name from an old sea captain in the early 1800s. He would "haul over" his boat from Biscayne Bay, across a narrow strip of land, to the ocean.

Have you ever gone fishing and felt a tug at the end of your line? Well, Miami has many places where you can try your luck at fishing. It is right on the Atlantic Ocean.

A great place is **Haulover Park** on the north end of Miami Beach. There's a pier nearby where you can rent a rod and tackle, buy bait, and get good advice from experienced anglers.

You can take a charter boat and try for kingfish, mackerel, snapper, grouper, and more. The mates on board will help you bait your hook, give you a hand when you catch something, and even clean and fillet the fish if you want to take it home and cook it.

MY TRAVEL JOURNAL
—Good Sports—

I had fun when I visited: _____

My favorite sport is: _____

I like it because: _____

This is a picture of something I saw

6 MUSEUMS AND MORE

THERE'S A LOT TO DO, EVEN ON A RAINY DAY in Miami. You can conduct experiments at the Museum of Science, "drive" a fire engine at the Youth Museum, or pretend to be a pilot at the Weeks Air Museum.

At most museums in Miami, you won't just stand around and look at displays. You will touch, push, build, and try out all kinds of exhibits and activities. Some of the things you will see are old (Indian and pirate artifacts), and some are new (computers and airplanes). The Museum of Science has had special exhibits on dinosaurs and shipwrecks. The Historical Museum has displayed a ship that brought slaves from Africa more than 300 years ago.

The Miami Art Museum has programs just for kids.

Museums and More

❶ American Police Hall of Fame and Museum
❷ Historical Museum of Southern Florida
❸ Lowe Art Museum
❹ Miami Art Museum
❺ Miami Museum of Science
❻ Miami Youth Museum
❼ Weeks Air Museum

MIAMI MUSEUM OF SCIENCE

Do you want to test your balance and strength, touch a box turtle, and watch a skeleton ride a bicycle? Do you want to hear what a hurricane sounds like? You can do all that and more at the Miami Museum of Science.

You can take a picture of your own shadow, measure your arm strength, and test your skill on a balancing board. Exhibits show how the human body works, from how we hear sounds to how we ride bikes.

The **Planetarium** at the museum has laser and star shows at night. It's next door to **Vizcaya**, a huge mansion with beautiful gardens and secret pathways.

⇡ How does an arch stay standing? You'll find out at the Miami Museum of Science.

In the back of the science museum is a small wildlife rehabilitation center. There, you can see scientists care for injured ospreys and other birds of prey.

WEATHER WORD GAME

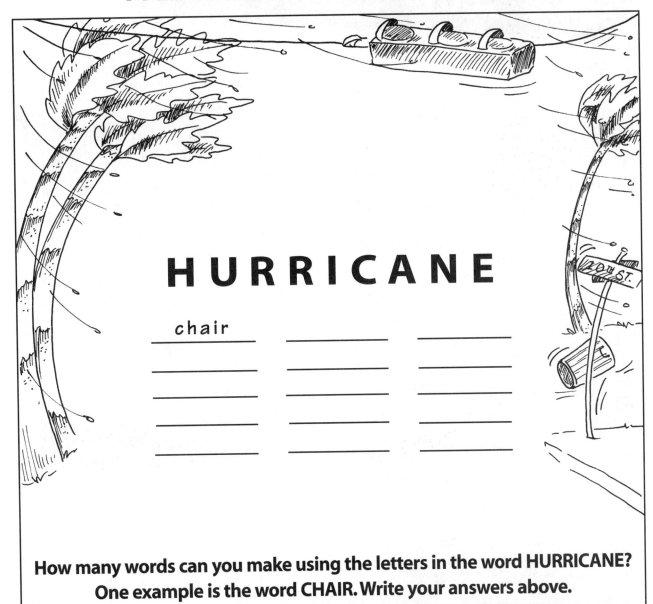

HURRICANE

chair
_____ _____ _____
_____ _____ _____
_____ _____ _____
_____ _____ _____
_____ _____ _____

How many words can you make using the letters in the word HURRICANE?
One example is the word CHAIR. Write your answers above.

MIAMI YOUTH MUSEUM

The Miami Youth Museum is a great place for make-believe. It has a pretend supermarket, fire truck, and TV station—all designed for kids. You can slide down a fire pole, appear on television, or put on your own puppet show. The museum also puts on plays and other special events.

The museum is in **Paseos**, a mall that also has movie theaters, music and clothing stores, and **Play City**, a place to climb rope ladders and explore tunnels. Play City also has snacks and video games.

⇑ **Kids run the show at the Miami Youth Museum TV station.**

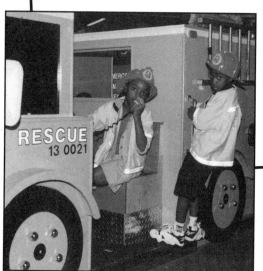

⇐ **Young firemen to the rescue!**

Do you want to learn how to cook pancakes, Mexican food, or other meals? Often on Saturdays, the Youth Museum has cooking classes just for kids.

GEOGRAPHY QUIZ

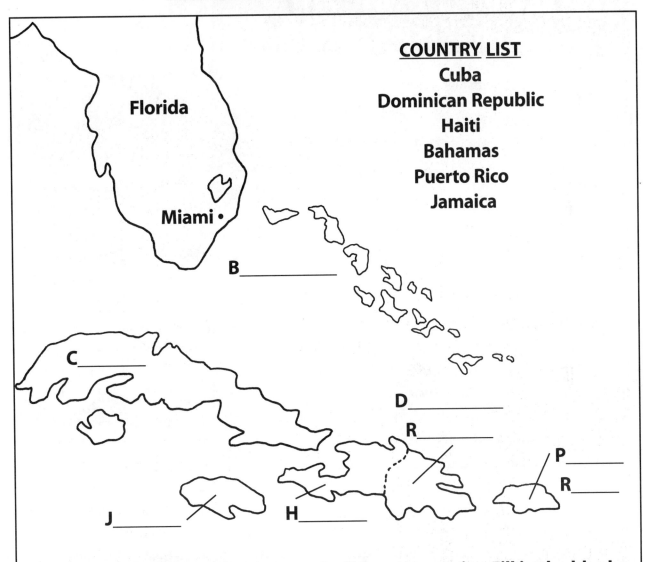

COUNTRY LIST
Cuba
Dominican Republic
Haiti
Bahamas
Puerto Rico
Jamaica

Florida

Miami •

B_____

C_____

D_____

R_____

P_____

R_____

J_____

H_____

People come to Miami from many Caribbean countries. Fill in the blanks to match each country with its correct place on the map.

HISTORICAL MUSEUM OF SOUTHERN FLORIDA

A few hundred years ago there were few people in southern Florida and no big buildings. The Historical Museum of Southern Florida shows you what life was like back then. It teaches you how Seminole Indians fished from flat-bottom boats and where pirates tried to hide their treasure.

You can touch the tools that pioneers used, and maybe try on some of their clothes. You can also step aboard one of the first trolley cars in Miami and see what's left of shipwrecked boats.

The museum has a great store with T-shirts, jewelry, and souvenirs. Make sure you call ahead to find out about the exhibits.

⬆ See a colonial cannon and more.

Have you ever slept in a museum? Sometimes the Historical Museum holds sleepovers. You can spend the whole night near pirate gear and Indian boats.

HIDDEN TREASURE

Pirates are not very common anymore. But it looks like some pirates have shown up to find a hidden treasure chest. Can you find the hidden treasure before the pirates do? Circle the treasure, then color the scene.

WEEKS AIR MUSEUM

Maybe you came to Miami on a large jet aircraft. That's very different from the airplanes you will see at the Weeks Air Museum next to Tamiami Airport south of Miami.

There are fighter planes from World War II, a time before jets were made. You can look inside the cockpit of a B-29 bomber or check out a P-51 Mustang, planes that fought battles with other planes during the war.

You can also touch old engine parts and propellers. You can buy souvenirs in the gift shop. Every year the museum has an art and photo contest. The best pictures of airplanes get prizes.

⇡ **Old propeller planes and others are on display.**

Many of the aircraft at Weeks are in flying condition. Every year some of the planes are flown at special shows. Pilots fly old bombers and fighter planes from other places in for the events.

MATCH THE PLANES

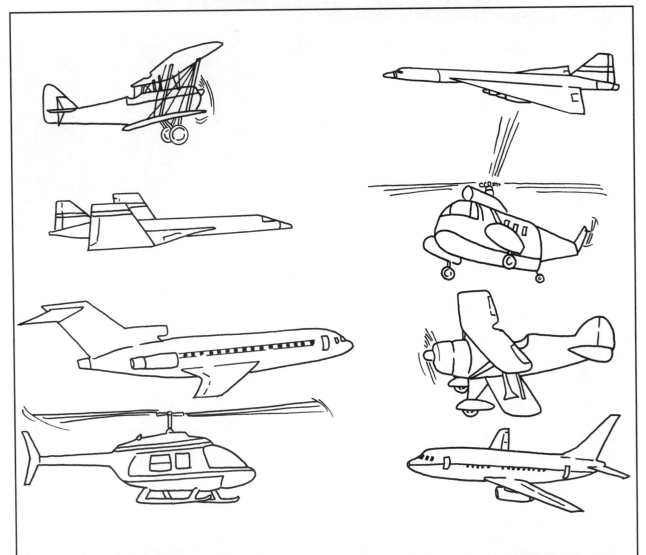

There are many different kinds of aircraft. Find the craft on the left that matches one on the right. Connect the matching pictures with a line.

MIAMI ART MUSEUM

A hide-and-seek game? That's just one of the things you will find at the Miami Art Museum, which is in downtown Miami next to the Historical Museum of South Florida.

When you enter one of the galleries, look for a guidebook that shows different shapes. Then try to find those shapes in different paintings and sculptures. Most Saturday afternoons there are tours designed for families. You can watch videos of artists at work, and you are allowed to sketch anywhere in the museum. After you see the museum, visit the shaded picnic area on the plaza outside.

⇧ **The art museum is a place to learn and have fun.**

⇧ **Snack time at the museum**

YOU BE THE ARTIST!

Many artists live in Miami. You can be an artist, too. On the blank canvas, draw a picture of something you've seen on your trip.

AMERICAN POLICE HALL OF FAME AND MUSEUM

⇑ **Kids try out the stocks, which held prisoners in colonial days.**

↗ **Pretend you're a motorcycle cop.**

You know you're approaching an unusual museum when you see vehicles that look like tanks—with armor and battering rams—parked outside. And on the outside of the building, a police car appears to be driving down the wall.

The American Police Hall of Fame and Museum is dedicated to police officers and crime fighting. Inside you'll find a futuristic police car from the movie *Blade Runner*, weapons, and collections of badges, patches, and hats from officers around the world.

The museum has exhibits about how the police caught some bad guys, such as gangsters in the 1930s. There's even a pretend crime scene with clues. If you can solve the crime, you get a certificate. The museum also has a memorial to officers killed on the job.

DETECTIVE WORK!

Hidden in this word search are some words that have to do with crime fighting. Search for words vertically, horizontally, and diagonally. Can you find all 9 words? One word has been found for you.

Word Box

cop	jail
crime	evidence
gun	uniform
badge	clue
gangster	

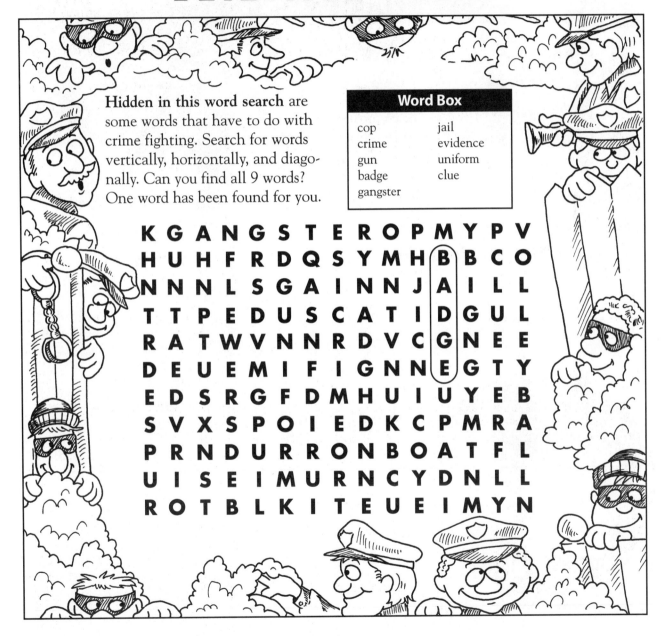

```
K G A N G S T E R O P M Y P V
H U H F R D Q S Y M H B B C O
N N N L S G A I N N J A I L L
T T P E D U S C A T I D G U L
R A T W V N N R D V C G N E E
D E U E M I F I G N N E G T Y
E D S R G F D M H U I U Y E B
S V X S P O I E D K C P M R A
P R N D U R R O N B O A T F L
U I S E I M U R N C Y D N L L
R O T B L K I T E U E I M Y N
```

LOWE ART MUSEUM

Lowe Art Museum has lots of different kinds of art, from Haitian flags made of sequins to a child's bonnet and moccasins made by Plains Indians. When you walk in, you'll see a tired-looking football player sitting on his helmet. He looks very lifelike, but get closer—he's a sculpture! Look for the horse named Rex, constructed from pieces of steel.

On some Sundays, the museum has kids' programs, with storytelling, games, and artwork. You can draw shapes like Pablo Picasso did, or make an African mask. The Lowe Museum store has interesting instruments, such as drums from Haiti and other Caribbean islands.

Nearby, at **Coral Gables City Hall**, a farmers' market operates Saturday mornings from January through March.

⇑ **You never know who, or what, you'll meet at the farmers' market at Coral Gables.**

Books and Books, a Coral Gables bookstore, sponsors kids' programs many Saturdays. You might see a play, check out a fire engine, or even get a visit from "The Wild Thing."

⇐ **Face painting at Lowe Art Museum**

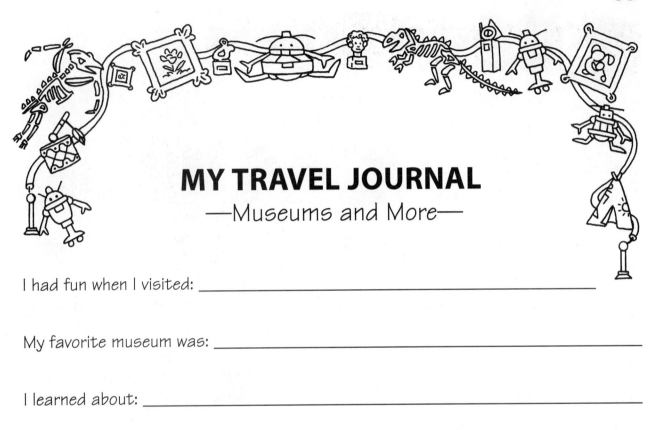

MY TRAVEL JOURNAL
—Museums and More—

I had fun when I visited: _____

My favorite museum was: _____

I learned about: _____

This is a picture of a painting or sculpture I saw

NEARBY AND NEAT

IF YOU'RE TRAVELING AROUND south Florida in a car, there are lots of great places just a short drive away.

Broward County, to the north of Miami, has some good beaches. The beach in Hollywood, close to Miami, has a paved boardwalk and arcades filled with games.

At the science museum in Fort Lauderdale, you'll get into the swing of things!

Just north of Hollywood is Fort Lauderdale, which has a beautiful beach and a new development of shops, restaurants, and movie theaters. The Museum of Discovery and Science is worth visiting. So is nearby Butterfly World.

About 50 miles south of Miami you enter the Florida Keys, hundreds of tiny islands linked by a single road called the Overseas Highway. There are many places in the Keys to swim, snorkel, camp, and fish.

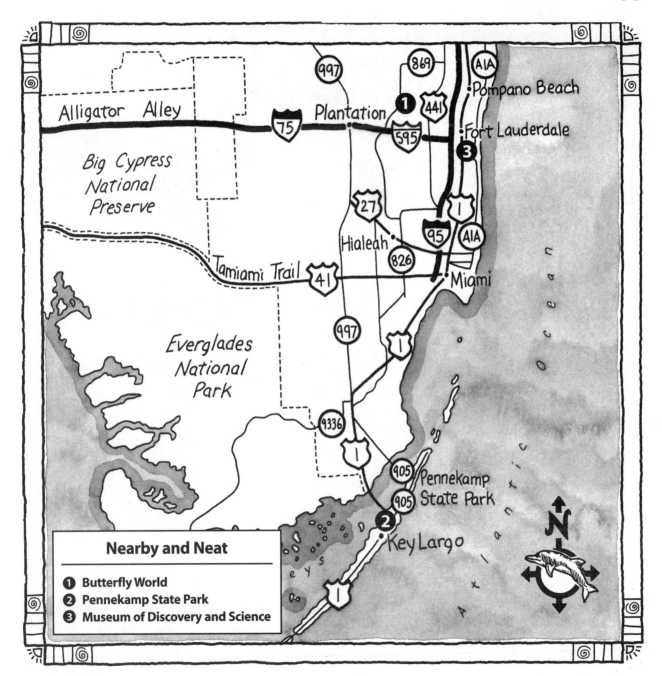

Nearby and Neat

1 **Butterfly World**
2 **Pennekamp State Park**
3 **Museum of Discovery and Science**

MUSEUM OF DISCOVERY AND SCIENCE

There's a spectacular museum, the Museum of Discovery and Science, in Fort Lauderdale. It's about 40 miles north of Miami—but it's worth the trip.

You'll notice something unusual at the museum entrance: a large sculpture with colored balls rolling around it. The sculpture is actually a clock that operates on gravity. Figuring out the time will be a challenge.

Inside there are high-tech exhibits on space, wildlife (how close can you get to a tarantula spider?), and a great gift shop.

The Blockbuster IMAX 3D theater (admission is extra) shows movies on a screen that's five-stories tall. You'll wear 3-D glasses that put you right in the movie. For example, you'll feel like you're flying a plane over New York City.

⇪ **Hands-on space exploration**

How hard would it be to land a spacecraft on the moon? You can find out when you pilot a simulator that's part of the museum's space exhibit.

BLAST OFF!

Many space voyages begin in Cape Canaveral, Florida, about 200 miles north of Miami. Imagine yourself on a voyage to outer space. Then color the scene.

BUTTERFLY WORLD

There's a special place just north of Fort Lauderdale where you can get close to nature. In fact, don't be surprised if nature—in the form of a beautiful butterfly—lands right on your shoulder.

Butterfly World has the largest display of live butterflies in the world. About 5,000 butterflies fly through the exhibit. If you're patient and stand still, a butterfly might land on you.

You can also visit a laboratory where caterpillars become butterflies. Watch as newborn butterflies emerge from their cocoons. The newborns are released several times a day.

Explore the Secret Garden, a mysterious, shaded maze with unusual flowers. At the museum gift shop you can buy plants that attract butterflies.

At Butterfly World you can watch hummingbirds smaller than your hand. Their wings move so quickly that they look like just a blur.

Butterflies and moths are everywhere...

...even on your shoulder!

HELP THE HUMMINGBIRD

START

FINISH

Hummingbirds love to sip nectar from flowers. Help this hummingbird fly through the maze to get to its favorite flowers.

PENNEKAMP STATE PARK

If you like swimming and sea life, Pennekamp State Park is the place for you. It was the first underwater park in the United States, and it includes part of one of the world's largest coral reef systems. The park is about 50 miles south of Miami.

You can take a glass-bottom boat out to the reef to see brightly colored parrotfish and needlefish up close. Sometimes a sleek barracuda or sand shark glides by.

You can rent a face mask, fins, and snorkel, then take a boat out to the reef. As you float on the surface looking down, you may feel like you're swimming in a big aquarium. You can also rent boats and fishing equipment.

⇑ **Snorkeling opens up a whole new world.**

Pennekamp State Park is in the Florida Keys—a string of tiny islands that stretch more than 100 miles into the Gulf of Mexico.

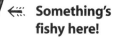

⇐ **Something's fishy here!**

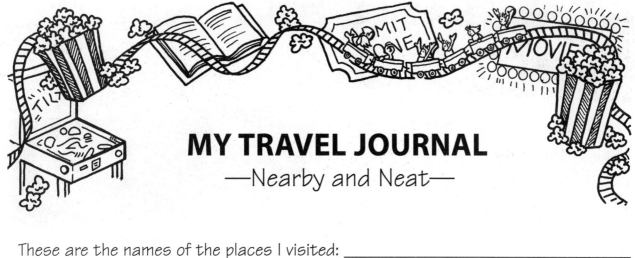

MY TRAVEL JOURNAL
—Nearby and Neat—

These are the names of the places I visited: _____

My favorite place was: _____

The strangest thing I saw was: _____

This is a picture of something I saw

8 THAT'S ENTERTAINMENT

THE BEST THING ABOUT MIAMI IS THE WARM weather. You can almost always do things outside here. But some days, especially in summer, heavy rains fall, and you have to look for something to do inside.

Fortunately, there are plenty of indoor places for fun in Miami. Malls, such as Bayside in downtown Miami, give you lots to do besides shopping. Many malls have playgrounds and special activities for kids.

There are also several places for indoor recreation, especially if you like in-line skating or roller skating. Even on the hottest rainy day in summer, you can grab a coat and go ice skating!

↥ **If you like plays, stop by the Actors' Playhouse in Coral Gables.**

Krome Av

Okeechobee Rd

Florida's Turnpike

HIALEAH

W 4th AV

E 8th AV

N MIAMI

NW 103rd St

NW 79th St

W 21st St

NW 36th St

Miami International Airport

NW 27th AV

Biscayne Blvd

❹

95

836

Collins Av

❷

MIAMI

MIAMI BEACH

997

Tamiami Trail

826

❶

LeJeune Rd

1

Rickenbacker Cswy

SW 157th AV

SW 137th AV

Bird Rd

KENDALL

Kendall Dr

❸

Don Shula Expwy

CORAL GABLES Hwy

Old Cutler Rd

S Dixie

Crandon Blvd

Key Biscayne

Biscayne Bay

Atlantic Ocean

SW 152nd St

Perrine

Quail Roost Dr

Cutler Ridge

Krome Av

SW 216th St

1

264th St

Bauer Dr

Florida's Turnpike

❺

Homestead

Homestead Air Force Base

Biscayne National Park Headquarters

Canal Dr

Florida City

Palm Dr

N

That's Entertainment

❶ **Actors' Playhouse**
❷ **Bayside Marketplace**
❸ **Hot Wheels Skating Center**
❹ **Miami Ice Arena**
❺ **Tropical Fun Center**

BAYSIDE MARKETPLACE

Bayside Marketplace is an indoor-outdoor group of stores and restaurants, right on the bay in downtown Miami. But there's more to do here than just shop. There's plenty of music—just look for the outdoor stage—and street performers. You'll even see people walking around with parrots and other animals.

There's a Disney store and a Warner Brothers store, and many places to buy souvenirs. There are lots of boats—from old schooners to powerboats—that can take you for a ride in the bay.

Next door to Bayside is a small park, **Bayfront**, with an amphitheater. Almost every weekend you can see free or inexpensive concerts there. There's often a festival celebrating the music and traditions of different ethnic groups.

⬆ **Bayside lights up at night.**

Some of the largest cruise ships in the world come into Miami just north of Bayside. You can get a good view of the ships from Watson Island, a short drive from Bayside.

CRUISIN'!

You'll see lots of cruise ships in Miami. This ship has some unlikely passengers, though. Circle the passengers who might be stowaways.

MIAMI ICE ARENA

Here's a trick question: Where can you find ice on a hot, rainy day in Miami?

The Miami Ice Arena, about 10 miles north of downtown, has a great rink, skates to rent, a snack bar, and a game room. You can rent a locker for just $1. But remember to bring a sweater or jacket, because it feels cold on the ice—especially when you've just come in from 90-degree weather outside.

Sometimes local hockey teams practice here, so make sure you call ahead for skating times. Afterward, you can go home and tell your friends you went ice skating when it was 90 degrees!

What's the most popular kids' sport in Miami? In some neighborhoods it's street hockey, played on in-line skates with hockey sticks and pads.

ICE MAGIC

Ice skating is a popular sport, even in Miami, where it's almost always warm. Beginning with the number 1, trace the skater's fancy footwork to uncover the hidden message.

ACTORS' PLAYHOUSE

Would you like the chance to watch a play and then meet the actors afterward? Would you like to ask the performers about their acting and singing? You can do that at the Actors' Playhouse in Coral Gables. The playhouse stages shows for kids most Saturday afternoons from November to August.

Ebenezer Scrooge may look scary from a distance, but up close he will sign autographs and tell you how he puts on his makeup. Along with *A Christmas Carol*, the Actors' Playhouse performs other shows such as *Cinderella*, *Once Upon a Shoe* (Mother Goose stories), and *King Midas and His Friends*.

Actors' Playhouse is one of the most famous places in the country for kids' theater. Some years, the playhouse hosts the National Children's Theatre Festival, with shows and actors from all over the United States.

⇡ **The Wizard of Oz is a favorite show for kids.**

WHAT'S THE DIFFERENCE?

These two theater scenes might look the same, but they are not.
How many differences between the two pictures can you find?
Hint: There are at least 10 differences.

HOT WHEELS SKATING CENTER

If you like in-line skating or roller skating, Hot Wheels Skating Center is a good place for you. You can rent all the equipment you'll need. There's a computerized light show and a DJ who plays popular music as you glide around the rink. There's also a large snack bar and a video arcade.

Sometimes the center hosts private parties, so always call ahead to check on skatings times. Hot Wheels is in the Kendall area, a busy neighborhood, and near two major shopping areas—Dadeland Mall and The Falls.

In-line skating has become so popular that new rinks are opening all the time around Miami. Rinks called **Thunder Wheels** recently opened west of the Miami Airport.

⬆ **Skaters on a roll!**

Be sure to wear a helmet and pads when you go skating. It's important to protect your head, elbows, knees, and hands.

FUN WITH WORDS

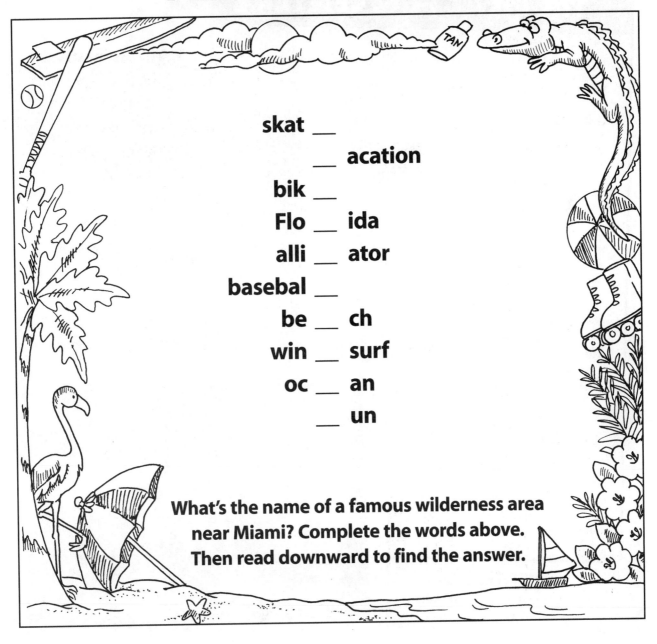

skat __

__ acation

bik __

Flo __ ida

alli __ ator

basebal __

be __ ch

win __ surf

oc __ an

__ un

What's the name of a famous wilderness area near Miami? Complete the words above. Then read downward to find the answer.

TROPICAL FUN CENTER

Let's say you spent part of the day exploring the Everglades and now you want to do something different. You might head to the Tropical Fun Center, which has an 18-hole miniature golf course, go-carts on a quarter-mile track, a game arcade, and a snack bar. Kids ages 3 to 9 can bounce around in a castle maze. The batting cages here have different pitching speeds and computerized scoring.

The Tropical Fun Center is in the town of Naranja (Spanish for "orange"), where many homes were destroyed by Hurricane Andrew in 1992. In the years afterward, many families moved away and there wasn't much for kids to do. So the whole community celebrated when the Fun Center opened a few years ago.

The Homestead Rodeo is held every winter not far from Naranja. It's a real Western rodeo, with bull-riding and calf-roping contests.

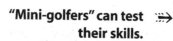
"Mini-golfers" can test their skills.

MY TRAVEL JOURNAL
—That's Entertainment—

These are the names of the places I visited: _____

My favorite place was: _____

The strangest thing I saw was: _____

This is a picture of something I saw

9 LET'S EAT!

MIAMI IS A CROSSROADS CITY, WITH PEOPLE from many cultures and countries—especially Haiti, Cuba, and other places in the Caribbean and Latin America. So eating in Miami gives you a chance to try lots of foods from foreign countries. And because Miami is on the water, you'll also get to eat lots of seafood.

Cuban food is tasty. Try *arroz con pollo* (chicken and rice) or *ropa vieja*. In Spanish, ropa vieja means "old clothes!" But it's not made of clothes, just bits of beef. For lunch, lots of places serve a Cuban sandwich, which is very tasty. It has thin strips of beef, pork, and cheese, and it's grilled in a machine that looks like a waffle iron.

↑ **It's fun to eat outside in Miami.**

Let's Eat

1. **Bayside**
2. **Café Tu Tu Tango**
3. **Monty Trainer's**
4. **Tap Tap**
5. **Versailles**

Gra

OPA-LOCKA

Opa-Locka Blvd

35th St
NW 119th St

NORTH MIAMI

W Dixie Hwy

Sunny Isles Blvd

Broad Cswy

NW 103rd St

HIALEAH

E 8th AV

Miami AV

Biscayne Blvd

Biscayne

I-95

John F Kennedy

NW 79th St

27th AV

Cswy

NW 62nd St

N

Bay

Airport Expressway

MIAMI

Julia Tuttle

Cswy

Venetian

Cswy

Collins AV

MIAMI BEACH

Okeechobee Rd

27

836

Dolphin Expwy

LeJeune Rd

W Flagler St

Mac Arthur Cswy

5

41 Trail

SW 37th NW

3 1

Dixie Hwy

Tamiami

Rickenbacker

4

Bird Rd

CORAL GABLES

2

S Bayshore Dr

Cswy

COCONUT GROVE

Crandon Blvd

KEY BISCAYNE

South

Ocean

Atlantic Ocean

TAP TAP

Have you ever eaten in a restaurant with huge murals and colorful paintings on the walls? Where even your table looks like a work of art?

Tap Tap is that kind of place. It's a Haitian restaurant on Miami Beach. Haitian people use many unusual ingredients in their meals—even goat! Yes, charcoal-grilled goat is on the menu. You'll also find plenty of foods you're used to, such as chicken, fish, and pork.

The fish and the meat dishes are spicy, but not too spicy. They come with rice and black beans or mushrooms. Try the homemade ginger ale (called ginger beer). And save room for a special dessert—sherbert in tropical fruit flavors, such as mango.

⬆ **Murals at Tap Tap can teach you about life in Haiti.**

Tap Tap gets its name from the colorful buses in Haiti, where drivers often tap their horns in traffic.

FOOD FAVORITES

YUM · YUM · YUM

Hidden in this puzzle are the names of foods you might eat in Miami. Search for words vertically, horizontally, and diagonally. One word has been found for you. Can you find all 10 words?

Word Box

chicken	ice cream	pork
beans	guava	shrimp
rice	fish	
mango	ginger ale	

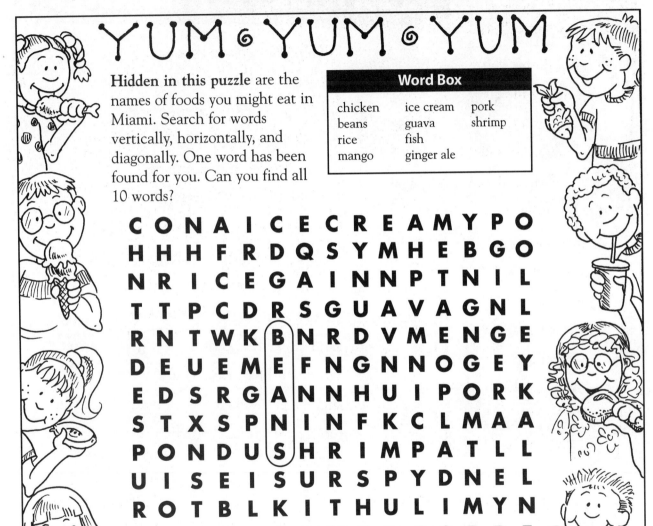

```
C O N A I C E C R E A M Y P O
H H H F R D Q S Y M H E B G O
N R I C E G A I N N P T N I L
T T P C D R S G U A V A G N L
R N T W K B N R D V M E N G E
D E U E M E F N G N N O G E Y
E D S R G A N N H U I P O R K
S T X S P N I N F K C L M A A
P O N D U S H R I M P A T L L
U I S E I S U R S P Y D N E L
R O T B L K I T H U L I M Y N
D Y D N I O P Y F R C S B R E
```

YUM · YUM · YUM

BAYSIDE RESTAURANT

⬆ **You can eat near the beach at Bayside.**

Looking for a place that Miami families know about, but not too many tourists? Bayside is a small restaurant with good seafood and hamburgers. It's very close to the beaches on Key Biscayne.

At Bayside Restaurant, you can peel some shrimp, munch on chicken, sip black bean soup, and get a great view of downtown Miami. Best of all, there's live music of all kinds on weekends. Nobody minds when kids get up and dance.

Bayside is off Rickenbacker Causeway, before you get to Seaquarium and Key Biscayne. All along the causeway there are places to rent sailboards. Ice cream and snack trucks park in the shade by the narrow beach.

On Hobie Beach along the causeway, you can rent more than just sailboards. You can rent hydrobikes, which you pedal in water, waterbikes, which have motors, and regular bikes.

AN OPEN BOOK!

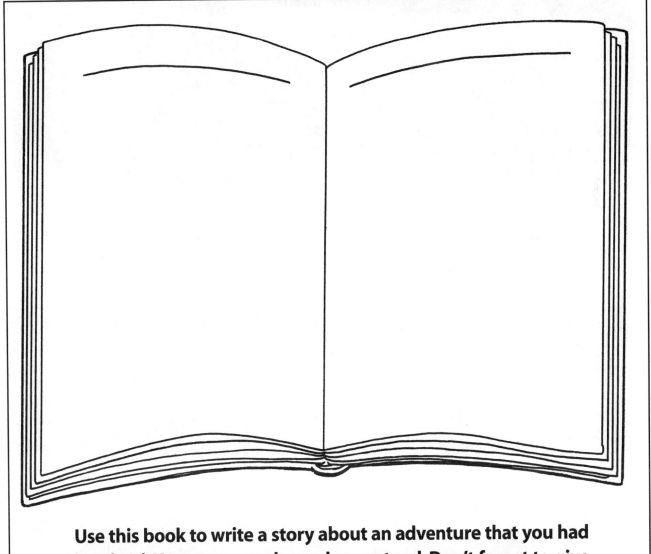

Use this book to write a story about an adventure that you had in Miami. Your story can be real or pretend. Don't forget to give your story a name. Write it on the top of the page.

VERSAILLES

Ready for some Cuban food? Versailles, a popular restaurant in **Little Havana** (Miami's Cuban neighborhood), will give you a good taste—and a full stomach. The portions are large and filling.

The waitresses, in green uniforms, are friendly. They enjoy it when you try speaking Spanish. They will help you make selections. Whether you order fish, beef, chicken, or pork, try the *frijoles negros* (black beans) that come with almost every meal. You might try a flaky guava pastry for dessert.

The Versailles is more than a restaurant for many Cuban immigrants. It is a home away from home, and a place for special events for the Cuban community.

⬆ **Give some Cuban food a try.**

Versailles was named for a famous palace outside Paris, France. Like the Versailles in France, the restaurant has many mirrors, but not as many.

SPANISH LESSON

Many people in Miami speak Spanish. Foods have Spanish names, too. Here are some common foods and their Spanish names. Try out these words when you order at a restaurant in Miami!

ENGLISH WORD	SPANISH WORD	PRONUNCIATION
rice	arroz	(AR-ros)
chicken	pollo	(POY-yoh)
beans	frijoles	(free-HO-lays)
pork	puerco	(PWEHR-koh)

The conch is actually a sea snail, belonging to the same family as clams, oysters, squids, and octopuses.

MONTY TRAINER'S

In Miami you can eat outdoors all year, and Monty Trainer's restaurant on Biscayne Bay in Coconut Grove is a great place to enjoy the weather. Even on a hot day, you can sit under a thatched hut with ceiling fans and feel a nice breeze.

At Monty's, you'll find familiar foods such as chicken fingers and nachos. But you might also want to try new foods, such as conch fritters. A conch is a small sea creature that lives inside a big shell. At Monty's the conch is deep fried in spicy batter. It's a favorite dish in the Bahamas, an island nation not far from Florida.

They often play Caribbean music at Monty's, and no one will mind if you get up and dance. Check out the boats of all sizes at the marina next door.

⇑ **You'll love the tropical surroundings at Monty Trainer's.**

HIDE AND SEEK

**These snorkelers are looking for animals under the water.
Help them look. How many animals can you find?**

CAFÉ TU TU TANGO

Have you ever eaten in a restaurant while artists worked nearby? You can at Café Tu Tu Tango. You can munch and watch painters hard at work. Sometimes there's live music, too. The restaurant is in Cocowalk, a popular shopping area in Coconut Grove.

Café Tu Tu Tango is special because all the portions are like appetizers. There are 41 items to choose from. You can try several small meat, fish, and vegetable dishes. They're easy to share. The restaurant also serves different kinds of pizza, including one with eggplant and tomato. Another pizza has chicken and cheddar cheese. Make sure you leave room for dessert. You might try the guava cheesecake with strawberry sauce.

Be careful when you reach for your drink at Tu Tu Tango. You might grab a cup filled with paintbrushes instead. They're all over the place.

⬆ **Café Tu Tu Tango looks almost like an artist's studio.**

MY TRAVEL JOURNAL
—Let's Eat!—

My favorite restaurant was: _____

The most unusual food I ate was: _____

My least favorite food was: _____

This is a picture of one restaurant I visited

CALENDAR OF MIAMI EVENTS

Because of the wonderful weather, there are many special events held outdoors in the Miami area. Many are ethnic events. Others are sporting contests. And there are indoor shows and exhibits whatever the weather.

Most events are held in the same month every year, or at least in the same season. Call ahead and learn more about each event and when it will be held.

January

Art Deco Weekend
Along Ocean Drive, Miami Beach, (305) 672-2014. This street festival in the heart of the Miami Beach historic district features food, music, arts, and crafts. Admission is free. The Design Preservation League also conducts biking and walking tours of the Art Deco district.

Taste of the Grove
Peacock Park, Coconut Grove, (305) 444-7270. This is a great chance to try some local foods such as conch fritters and *arroz con pollo*, prepared by chefs from some of the best restaurants in the grove.

Homestead Championship Rodeo
Harris Field, Homestead, (305) 247-3515. It's not the Wild West, but the Homestead Rodeo always has exciting competition in bull riding and other traditional events.

Redlands Natural Arts Festival
Fruit and Spice Park, Homestead, (305) 247-5727. Arts and crafts are on display at this small festival, which will give you a feel for life in rural Dade County.

February

Miami International Boat Show
Miami Beach Convention Center, (305) 531-8410. This is one of the biggest boat shows in the world, displaying everything from small sailboards to enormous yachts.

Coconut Grove Art Festival
Coconut Grove, (305) 447-0401. This festival, one of the largest outdoor art festivals in the country, brings hundreds of artists and craftspeople to the streets of Coconut Grove for three to four days. You can park in lots along Dixie Highway (U.S. 1) and take a shuttle bus.

Grand Prix of Miami
Metro-Dade Homestead Motorsports Complex, (305) 379-7223. This beautiful race track, finished a few years ago, has several big races each year. The Marlboro Grand Prix is the biggest and most popular.

March

Calle Ocho Festival
On SW 8th Street (the heart of Little Havana) between 4th and 27th Avenues, (305) 644-8888. This just might be the biggest block party around.

Actually you'll find 23 blocks of food, music, and dancing in celebration of Cuban culture. Thousands of people attend every year.

Doral-Ryder Open
Doral Golf Resort and Spa, (305) 477-4653. If you like golf, this is the place to be in early March. The tournament attracts great golfers.

Lipton Tennis Championships
Crandon Park Tennis Center, Key Biscayne, (305) 442-3367. This ten-day tournament is the biggest of the year, with most of the big-name pros playing. There are also interactive games and exhibits.

Italian Renaissance Festival
Vizcaya Museum and Gardens, Coconut Grove, (305) 250-9133. At this festival, step back in time to the days of medieval knights. There are jousting contests, plays, music, and often a chess match played with real knights and queens on a large board.

April

Dade County Youth Fair and Expostition
Tamiami Park, (305) 223-7060. The Youth Fair includes a huge amusement park with every kind of ride and a chance for Miami kids to show off their artwork, animals, and other projects. There's also lots of music and food.

Springtime Harvest Festival
Tamiami Park, (305) 987-4275. A small festival of food and music that celebrates the area's rich farming tradition.

Merrick Festival
Ponce Circle Park, Coral Gables, (305) 447-9299.

A small festival that's fun for kids. You'll enjoy skits, music, and lots of food from restaurants in Coral Gables.

Florida Marlins Home Opener
Pro Player Stadium, North Dade, (305) 523-3309. Join in the springtime festivities as the Marlins begin another season. The home opener is usually in early April. (Marlins games in April and May can be more enjoyable than those in the hot days of summer.)

May

Coconut Grove Bed Race
Peacock Park in Coconut Grove, (305) 624-3714. This is one of the strangest races you will ever see. Each year, to raise money for charities, teams race beds on wheels through the streets of the Grove.

Great Sunrise Balloon Race
Homestead Air Force Base, (305) 596-9040. You have to get up early for this one. But it's a gorgeous sight when dozens of colorful hot air balloons take to the skies in the early morning.

Arabian Nights Festival
Opa-locka City Hall grounds, (305) 688-4611. With its minarets and domes, the city hall at Opa-locka looks like it came from ancient Arabia. The festival celebrates this small town's unusual history.

Miami River Boat Tour
Along the Miami River, downtown Miami, (305) 375-1625. The river is always buzzing with activity. You'll be surprised at the large freighters that can navigate this narrow river. This tour gives you a chance to cruise the river and see the boats in action.

June

Miami/Bahamas Goombay Festival

Downtown Coconut Grove, (305) 372-9966. Celebrate Miami's Bahamian connection during a weekend festival. A highlight is Bahamian musicians, including a police band, complete with whistles and batons.

South Florida Boat Show

Miami Beach Convention Center, (305) 946-6164. This show isn't as big as the international one in February. But it's also not as crowded and still has lots of boats.

July

Fourth of July Celebrations

Amphitheater at Bayfront Park, downtown Miami, (305) 358-7550. There are several good locations in Miami for music and fireworks, but this is the biggest. It's next to Bayside Marketplace on Biscayne Bay.

Tropical Agriculture Fiesta

Fruit and Spice Park, Homestead. Here's a chance to try the great produce of south Dade County, including some exotic vegetables such as the papaya and malanga. There's also Mexican food and music.

August

Miami Reggae Festival

Amphitheater at Bayfront Park, downtown Miami, (305) 891-2944. This festival lets you sample Jamaican culture and food, including meat pies and jerk chicken. The beat of reggae music is very hard to resist.

Football Training Camp

Miami Dolphins Camp, Davie, (954) 452-7000. August can be the hottest month in Florida, and that's when football players sweat to get in shape. If you're a fan, this is a great way to see the players up close.

September

Festival Miami

University of Miami School of Music, Coral Gables, (305) 284-3941. This university's music school is one of the best in the country, and in August the students put on all sorts of concerts.

October

Hispanic Heritage Festival

Various locations throughout Dade County, (305) 541-5023. This is a celebration of Hispanic culture from many countries. Cuba, Nicaragua, and Colombia are just some of them. The month-long celebration features concerts, plays, and food.

Columbus Day Regatta

In Biscayne Bay, (305) 876-0818. This is the biggest sailing event of the year, with races from downtown, past Key Biscayne, to the north end of

Biscayne National Park. Rickenbacker Causeway on the way to Key Biscayne is a good place for watching the flotilla of sailboats.

West Indian Carnival Extravaganza

South Pointe Park, Miami Beach, (305) 435-4845. Haven't you always wanted to try curried goat? You'll get your chance at this festival of Caribbean food, music, and culture.

November

South Florida International Auto Show

Miami Beach Convention Center, (305) 758-2643. This huge display of all sorts of vehicles draws thousands of people to south Florida.

Banyan Arts and Crafts Festival

Downtown Coconut Grove, (305) 444-7270. Local artists and craftspeople, and some from far away, show off their works. This festival is a great chance to pick up some gifts for the holidays.

Miami International Book Fair

Miami-Dade Community College, downtown Miami, (305) 237-3258. Each year this book fair gets bigger and better. Look for the Children's Alley, which has all sorts of plays, music, shows, and attractions. Watch some of your favorite book characters come to life.

South Miami Art Festival

Along Sunset Drive, South Miami, (305) 661-1621. At this festival, you can walk around and see arts and crafts without big crowds.

December

Fairchild Tropical Garden Ramble

Fairchild Tropical Garden, Coral Gables, (305) 667-1651. You can visit a tropical paradise and purchase all sorts of flowers and plants. You can even find rare orchids here.

Miccosukee Tribe's Indian Arts Festival

Miccosukee Indian Village, on Tamiami Trail, 30 miles west of Miami, (305) 223-8380. Ride an airboat, get close to an alligator, and learn about the Miccosukee Indians at this weekend festival.

Junior Orange Bowl Parade

Downtown Coral Gables, (305) 662-1210. This parade is designed especially for kids. It's not quite as big or crowded as the parade downtown a few days later, so it's easy to get a good view. Look for a surprise visit from Santa Claus.

Orange Bowl Parade

Along Biscayne Boulevard, downtown Miami, (305) 371-4600. This is one of the great old-fashioned New Year's parades, with enormous floats and marching bands. It's usually held New Year's Eve, but not always. You can buy tickets and watch from bleachers along Biscayne Boulevard, or watch for free from a side street.

On New Year's Eve there's a celebration in Bayfront Park, with a "big orange" falling from a nearby building at midnight.

RESOURCE GUIDE: WHEN, WHAT, AND WHERE?

Here is a listing of the sights mentioned in this book, plus other places in and around Miami of interest to children and families. Hours and days of operation are subject to change, so be sure to call before you visit.

All the places in this Resource Guide have activities for kids and families. But not every activity or program at every place is suitable for kids. Before you buy tickets or attend an event, have your parents check to make sure the event is right for you.

If You Get Lost

It's a good idea to make a plan with your parents about what to do if you lose them. If you get lost while you're visiting one of Miami's parks or beaches, go to a uniformed park ranger or lifeguard. A police officer can help, too. If you're in a store or restaurant, go to the person working behind the cash register. If you're outside and don't see a ranger or police officer, find a mother with children and tell her you're lost.

In an emergency, you can dial 911 from any phone. You won't need money to do this, even at a pay phone. Only dial 911 if you need the police, fire department, or an ambulance.

Important Numbers

Injury, accident, or emergency, 911
Metro-Dade Fire and Police, (305) 595-6263
Miami Police Department, (305) 579-6640
Miami Beach Police Department, (305) 673-7900
Florida Highway Patrol, (305) 470-2500

Visitor Information

Greater Miami Convention and Visitors Bureau, 701 Brickell Avenue, Suite 2700, Miami, FL 33131; (800) 283-2707.
Miami Beach Chamber of Commerce, 1920 Meridian Avenue, Miami Beach, FL 33140; (305) 672-1270.

Transportation

Miami International Airport, (305) 876-7000
SuperShuttle (airport transfers), (305) 871-8210
Water Taxi (serves attractions on Biscayne Bay),
    (305) 467-6677
Metrorail and Metromover, (305) 638-6700
Flamingo Taxi, (305) 885-7000
Metro Taxi, (305) 888-8888
Amtrak, (305) 835-1222
Tri-Rail, fares, and schedules, (305-874-7245)

Attractions

Actors' Playhouse, 280 Miracle Mile, Coral
Gables, FL 33134; (305) 444-9293; Children's
shows Saturday at 2:00 p.m.

American Police Hall of Fame and Museum,
3801 Biscayne Boulevard, Miami, FL 33137; (305)
573-0070; Open daily, 10:00 a.m.–5:30 p.m.

Ancient Spanish Monastery, 16711 W. Dixie
Highway, North Miami Beach, FL 33160; (305)
945-1462; Open Monday through Saturday,
10:00 a.m.–4:00 p.m.; Sunday, noon to 4:00 p.m.

Art Deco Historic District, P.O. Box 190180,
1001 Ocean Drive, Miami Beach, FL 33119; (305)
672-2014. Information, walking, and bike tours.

Barnacle State Historic Site, 3485 Main Highway,
Coconut Grove, Fl 33133; (305) 448-9445. Open
daily, 9 a.m.–4 p.m.

Bass Museum of Art, 2121 Park Avenue, Miami
Beach, FL 33139; (305) 673-7530. Open Tuesday
through Saturday, 10:00 a.m.–5:00 p.m.; Sunday
1:00 p.m.–5:00 p.m.

Bayfront Park, 301 N. Biscayne Boulevard, Miami,
FL 33132; (305) 358-7550. Call for concert and
festival times.

Bayside Marketplace, 401 Biscayne Boulevard,
Miami, FL 33132; (305) 577-3344. Open Monday
through Thursday, 10:00 a.m.–10:00 p.m.; Friday
and Saturday, 10:00 a.m.–11:00 p.m.; Sunday,
11:00 a.m.–8:00 p.m. Many restaurants stay open
later.

Bayside Restaurant, 3501 Rickenbacker Causeway,
Miami, FL 33149; (305) 361-0808. Open for lunch
and dinner.

Bill Baggs Cape Florida State Park, 1200 S.
Crandon Park Boulevard, Key Biscayne, FL; (305)
361-5811. Open daily, 8:00 a.m. to sunset.

Biscayne National Park, P.O. Box 1369, Homestead, FL 33090; (305) 230-PARK. Most facilities open 8:30 a.m.–4:30 p.m.

Books and Books, 296 Aragon Avenue, Coral Gables, FL 33134; (305) 442-4408; and 933 Lincoln Road, Miami Beach, FL 33139; (305) 532-3222.

Butterfly World, Tradewinds Park South, 3600 W. Sample Road, Coconut Creek, FL 33073; (954) 977-4400. Open Monday through Saturday, 9:00 a.m.–5:00 p.m.; Sunday, 1:00 p.m.–5:00 p.m.

Café Tu Tu Tango, 3015 Grand Avenue, Miami FL; 33133; (305) 529-2222. Open for lunch and dinner.

CocoWalk, 3015 Grand Avenue, Miami, FL 33133; (305) 444-0777. Open Sunday through Thursday, 11:00 a.m.–10:00 p.m.; Friday and Saturday until midnight. Restaurants stay open late.

Color Me Mine, 3411 Main Highway, Coconut Grove, FL 33133; (305) 447-0809; open Monday through Thursday, 11:00 a.m.–9:00 p.m., Friday and Saturday, 11:00 a.m. to midnight. Sunday, noon to 9 p.m.

Coopertown Airboat Rides, 22700 SW 8th Street, Miami, FL 33194; (305) 226-6048; open daily, 8:00 a.m.–7:00 p.m.

Coral Castle, 28655 S. Dixie Highway (U.S. 1), Homestead, FL 33030; (305) 248-6344. Open daily, 9:00 a.m.–6 p.m.

Coral Gables Farmers Market, Merrick Park, 405 Biltmore Way, Coral Gables, FL; (305) 460-5310. Open Saturday from 10:00 a.m., January through March.

Crandon Park Beach, 4000 Crandon Boulevard, Key Biscayne, FL; (305) 361-5421. Open daily, 8:00 a.m. to sunset.

Everglades Alligator Farm, 40351 SW 192nd Avenue, Homestead, FL 33090; (305) 247-2628. Open daily, 9:00 a.m.–6:00 p.m.

Everglades National Park, 40001 State Road 9336, Homestead, FL 33090; (305) 242-7700. Most facilities open daily from 8:00 a.m.–5:00 p.m.

Fairchild Tropical Garden, 10901 Old Cutler Road, Miami FL 33156; (305) 667-1651. Open daily, 9:30 a.m.–4:30 p.m.

The Falls Shopping Center, S. Dixie Highway at SW 136th Street, Miami, FL 33176; (305) 247-5727; Open Monday through Saturday, 10:00 a.m.–5:00 p.m.; Sunday, noon to 5:00 p.m.

Florida Marlins, Pro Player Stadium, 2269 NW 199th Street, Miami, FL 33056; (305) 626-7400.

Florida Panthers, Miami Arena, 701 Arena Boulevard, Miami, FL 33136; (305) 530-4444.

Fruit and Spice Park, 24801 SW 187 Avenue, Homestead, FL 33031; (305) 247-5727. Open daily, 10:00 a.m.–5:00 p.m.

Haulover Marine Center, 1500 Collins Avenue, Miami Beach, FL 33154; (305) 945-3934.

Historical Museum of Southern Florida, 101 W. Flagler Street, Miami, FL 33130; (305) 375-1492. Open Monday through Saturday, 10:00 a.m.–5:00 p.m.; Thursday, 10:00 a.m.–9:00 p.m.; Sunday, noon to 5:00 p.m.

Hot Wheels Skating Center, 12265 SW 112th Street, Miami, FL 33186; (305) 595-2958. Open Tuesday and Wednesday, 3:00 p.m.–5:30 p.m.; Thursday, 4:30–5:30 p.m.; Friday, 3:00–6:00 p.m.; Saturday and Sunday, 11:30 a.m. on.

Lincoln Road Shopping District, 924 Lincoln Road, Miami Beach, FL 33139; (305) 531-3442.

Lowe Art Museum, University of Miami campus, 1301 Stanford Drive, Coral Gables, FL 33124; (305) 284-3535. Open Tuesday, Wednesday, Friday, and Saturday, 10:00 a.m.–5:00 p.m.; Thursday, noon to 7:00 p.m.; Sunday noon to 5:00 p.m.

Matheson Hammock Park, 9610 Old Cutler Road, Miami, FL 33156; (305) 666-6979. Open daily, 9:00 a.m.–4:30 p.m. Admission is $3.50 per car.

Metrozoo, 12400 SW 152 Street, Miami, FL 33177; (305) 251-0400. Open daily, 9:30 a.m.–5:30 p.m.

Miami Art Museum of Dade County, 101 W. Flagler Street, Miami, FL 33130; (305) 375-1700; Open Tuesday through Friday, 10:00 a.m.–5:00 p.m.; Saturday and Sunday, noon to 5:00 p.m.; closed Monday.

Miami City Ballet Studios, 905 Lincoln Road, Miami Beach, FL 33139; (305) 532-7713.

Miami Dolphins, Pro Player Stadium, 2269 NW 199th Street, Miami, FL 33056; (954) 452-7000 or (305) 620-2578.

Miami Heat, One SE 3rd Avenue, Suite 2300, Miami, FL 33131; (305) 577-4328.

Miami Ice Arena, 14770 Biscayne Boulevard, North Miami Beach, FL 33181; (305) 940-8222. Hours change during the year; usually 10:00 a.m.–5:00 p.m. on weekends.

Miami Museum of Science and Space Transit Planetarium, 3280 S. Miami Avenue, Miami, FL 33129; (305) 854-4247. Open daily, 10:00 a.m.–6:00 p.m.

Miami Seaquarium, 4400 Rickenbacker Causeway, Miami FL 33149; (305) 361-5705. Open daily, 9:30 a.m.–6:00 p.m.

Miami Youth Museum at Paseos, Level U, 3301 Coral Way, Miami, FL 33145; (305) 446-4386. Open Monday through Thursday, 10:00 a.m.–5:00 p.m.; Friday, 10:00 a.m.–9 p.m.; Saturday and Sunday, 11:00 a.m.–6:00 p.m.

Miccosukee Indian Village and Airboat Tours, P.O. Box 440021, Miami, FL 33144; (305) 223-8380. Open daily, 9:00 a.m.–5:00 p.m.

Monkey Jungle, 14805 SW 216th Street, Miami, FL 33170; (305) 235-1611. Open daily, 9:30 a.m.–5:00 p.m.

Monty Trainer's Restaurant and Raw Bar, 2550 S. Bayshore Drive, Coconut Grove, FL 33137; (305) 858-1431. Open for lunch and dinner.

Museum of Discovery and Science/Blockbuster IMAX 3D Theater, 401 SW 2nd Street, Fort Lauderdale, FL 33312; (954) 467-6637. Open Monday through Saturday, 10:00 a.m.–5:00 p.m.; Sunday, noon to 6:00 p.m.

New World Symphony, Lincoln Theatre, 541 Lincoln Road, Miami Beach, FL 33139; (305) 673-3331.

Parrot Jungle and Gardens, 11000 SW 57th Avenue, Miami FL 33156; (305) 666-7834. Open daily, 9:30 a.m.–6:00 p.m.

Pennekamp State Park, Mile Marker 102.5, Key Largo, FL 33037; (305) 451-1202. Open daily, 8 a.m. to sunset.

Robert Is Here fruit stand, 19900 SW 344th Street, Homestead, FL 33034; (305)246-1592.

South Florida Art Center, 924 Lincoln Road, Miami Beach, FL 33139; (305) 674-8278. Open daily, 9:00 a.m.–5 p.m.

Tap Tap Restaurant, 819 Fifth Street, Miami Beach; (305) 376-3447. Open for lunch and dinner.

Thunder Wheels, 8348 NW 103rd Street, Miami, FL 33016; (305) 824-5016 and 11401 W. Flagler Street, Miami, FL 33174; (305) 226-0074. Open daily, call for hours.

Tropical Fun Center, 27201 S. Dixie Highway, Naranja, FL 33032; (305) 246-3731. Open Monday through Thursday, 10:00 a.m.–10:00 p.m.; Friday through Sunday, 10:00 a.m. to midnight.

Venetian Pool, 2701 DeSoto Boulevard, Coral Gables, FL 33134; (305) 460-5356. Open Saturday and Sunday, 10:00 a.m.–4:30 p.m.; Tuesday through Friday, 11:00 a.m.–5:30 p.m.; closed Monday.

Versailles Restaurant, 3555 SW 8th Street, Miami, FL 33135; (305) 444-0240. Open for lunch and dinner.

Vizcaya Museum and Gardens, 3251 S. Miami Avenue, Miami, FL 33129; (305) 250-9133. Open daily, 9:30 a.m.–5:00 p.m.

Weeks Air Museum, Tamiami Airport, 14710 SW 128th Street, Miami, FL 33196; (305) 233-5197. Open daily, 10:00 a.m.–5:00 p.m.

The Wolfsonian, 1001 Washington Avenue, Miami Beach, FL 33139; (305) 531-1001. Open Tuesday through Saturday, 10:00 a.m.–6:00 p.m.; Sunday, noon to 5:00 p.m.

World Resources Restaurant, 719 Lincoln Road, Miami Beach, FL 33139; (305) 534-9095. Open for lunch and dinner.

ANSWERS TO PUZZLES

page 11

page 15

page 17

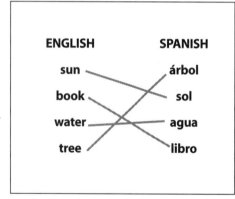

page 19

page
23

Here are some of the words you can make using the letters in the word **ALLIGATOR:**

page
25

at	grill	rot
all	ill	tag
art	it	tail
gill	log	tall
girl	rail	till
goal	rat	trail
goat	rig	
got	roll	

page
33

page
35

ALLIGATOR
BEAR
RACCOON
SNAKE
TURTLE

page
37

ACROSS

3. HURRICANE
5. FLORIDA
8. MIAMI

DOWN

1. SUN
2. FISHING
4. PALM
6. BEACH
7. RAINY

page
43

page 45

page 47

page 49

page 51

page 59

FINISH

START

page 61

page 63

```
B A S K E T M E S O P M Y P V
H P H F R D Q D Y M H E B A M
N Y O L S R A R N N J T S B L
T F O U L R E I A T I U G U L
R A T W G M N B D V C E M T R
D E U E M D F B O N N O G P Y
E P S R G B N L H U I U Y E B
S A X S P R I E D K N L M R A
P S N D U X R O W B O D U N K
U S H O O P U R N P Y D N E L
R O T B L K I T E U L I M T N
D Y D N I O P Y F H I S B E X
```

page 65

KAET	TAKE
EM	ME
UTO	OUT
OT	TO
ETH	THE
LMBAGALE	BALLGAME

page 71

Here are some of the words you can make using the letters in the word HURRICANE:

an	chin	rain
arch	crane	ran
are	each	ranch
can	ear	rare
cane	hen	rich
chain	her	ruin
chair	near	run

page 73

The Bahamas
Cuba
Haiti
Puerto Rico
Jamaica
Dominican Republic

page 75

page 77

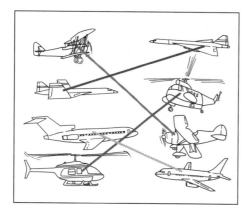

page 81

```
K G A N G S T E R O P M Y P V
H U H F R D Q S Y M H B B C O
N N L S G A I N N J A I L L
T T P E D U S C A T I D G U E
R A T W V N N R D V C G N E L
D E U E M I F I G N N E G T Y
E D S R G F D M H U I U Y E B
S V X S P O I E D K C P M R A
P R N D U R R O N B O A T F L
U I S E I M U R N C Y D N L L
R O T B L K I T E U E I M Y N
```

page 89

page 95

page 97

page 101

skat	E	
	V	acation
bik	E	
Flo	R	ida
alli	G	ator
basebal	L	
be	A	ch
win	D	surf
oc	E	an
	S	un

page 99

page 107

```
C O N A I C E C R E A M Y P O
H H H F R D Q S Y M H E B G O
N R I C E G A I N N P T N I L
T T P C D R S G U A V A G N L
R N T W K B N R D V M E N G E
D E U E M E F N G N N O G E Y
E D S R G A N N H U I P O R K
S T X S P N I N F K C L M A A
P O N D U S H R I M P A T L L
U I S E I S U R S P Y D N E L
R O T B L K I T H U L I M Y N
D Y D N I O P Y F R C S B R E
```

page 113

GEOGRAPHICAL INDEX: WHERE IS EVERYTHING?

INDEX:

American Origins Series

Each is 48 pages and $12.95 hardcover.
Tracing Our English Roots
Tracing Our German Roots
Tracing Our Irish Roots
Tracing Our Italian Roots
Tracing Our Japanese Roots
Tracing Our Jewish Roots
Tracing Our Polish Roots

Bizarre & Beautiful Series

Each is 48 pages, $14.95 hardcover, $9.95 paperback.
Bizarre & Beautiful Ears
Bizarre & Beautiful Eyes
Bizarre & Beautiful Feelers
Bizarre & Beautiful Noses
Bizarre & Beautiful Tongues

Extremely Weird® Series

Each is 32 pages and $5.95 paperback.
Extremely Weird Animal Defenses
Extremely Weird Animal Disguises
Extremely Weird Animal Hunters
Extremely Weird Bats
Extremely Weird Endangered Species
Extremely Weird Fishes
Extremely Weird Frogs
Extremely Weird Reptiles
Extremely Weird Spiders
Extremely Weird Birds
Extremely Weird Insects
Extremely Weird Mammals
Extremely Weird Micro Monsters
Extremely Weird Primates
Extremely Weird Sea Creatures
Extremely Weird Snakes

Kidding Around® Travel Series

Each is 144 pages and $7.95 paperback.
Kidding Around Atlanta
Kidding Around Austin
Kidding Around Boston
Kidding Around Cleveland
Kids Go! Denver
Kidding Around Indianapolis
Kidding Around Kansas City
Kidding Around Miami
Kidding Around Milwaukee
Kidding Around Minneapolis/St. Paul
Kidding Around San Francisco
Kids Go! Seattle
Kidding Around Washington, D.C.

Kids Explore Series

Written by kids for kids, each is $9.95 paperback.
Kids Explore America's African American Heritage, 160 pages
Kids Explore America's Hispanic Heritage, 160 pages
Kids Explore America's Japanese American Heritage, 160 pages
Kids Explore America's Jewish Heritage, 160 pages
Kids Explore Kids Who Make a Difference, 128 pages
Kids Explore the Gifts of Children with Special Needs, 128 pages
Kids Explore the Heritage of Western Native Americans, 128 pages

Rough and Ready Series

Each is 48 pages and $4.95 paperback.
Rough and Ready Homesteaders
Rough and Ready Cowboys
Rough and Ready Loggers
Rough and Ready Outlaws and Lawmen
Rough and Ready Prospectors
Rough and Ready Railroaders

X-ray Vision Series

Each is 48 pages and $6.95 paperback.
Looking Inside the Brain
Looking Inside Cartoon Animation
Looking Inside Caves and Caverns
Looking Inside Sports Aerodynamics
Looking Inside Sunken Treasure
Looking Inside Telescopes and the Night Sky

Ordering Information

Please check your local bookstore for our books, or call **1-800-888-7504** to order direct and to receive a complete catalog. A shipping charge will be added to your order total.

Send all inquiries to:
John Muir Publications
P.O. Box 613, Santa Fe, NM 87504

Butterfly World
Tradewinds Park South
3600 W. Sample Road
Coconut Creek, FL 33073
954-977-4400

$6.00 VALUE!

Expires 10/15/99

Buy one adult ticket and receive one child's ticket free. Not valid with any other discount offers.

**KIDDING AROUND®
MIAMI**

Hot Wheels Skating Center
12265 SW 112th St.
Miami, FL 33186
305-595-3200

$6.50 VALUE!

Expires 10/15/99

Buy one ticket and receive a second ticket free. Not valid for special events. Skate rental additional.

**KIDDING AROUND®
MIAMI**

American Police Hall of Fame and Museum
3801 Biscayne Boulevard
Miami, FL 33173
305-573-0070

TWO FOR THE PRICE OF ONE!

Expires 10/15/99

Buy one adult admission and receive a second admission of equal or lesser value free. Not valid with other discounts.

**KIDDING AROUND®
MIAMI**

Miami Youth Museum at Paseos
Level U, 3301 Coral Way
Miami, FL 33145
305-446-4386

TWO FOR THE PRICE OF ONE!

Expires 10/15/99

Buy one admission and receive a second admission free. Not valid with other discounts.

**KIDDING AROUND®
MIAMI**

The Wolfsonian
Florida International University
1001 Washington Avenue
Miami Beach, FL 33139
305-531-1001

$3.50 VALUE!

Expires 10/15/99

Valid for one free child's admission with one paid adult admission.

**KIDDING AROUND®
MIAMI**

Historical Museum of Southern Florida
101 W. Flagler Street
Miami, FL 33130
305-375-1492

$6.00 VALUE!

Expires 10/15/99

Free child's admission with one paid adult admission. Limit three children. Not valid with other discounts.

**KIDDING AROUND®
MIAMI**

coupons coupons coupons coupons coupons coupons coupons coupons coupons coupons coupons